Praise for **What to Read**

"Where else but in *What to Read* could you find such thought-ful, well-organized lists of recommended books? Mickey Pearl-man is a fine scholar and editor, and a reader to trust. She has done the readers of the world a real service with this book."
—**Angela Davis-Gardner**, author of *Forms of Shelter*

"This book is a wonderful idea, long overdue."
—**Margot Livesey**, author of *Learning By Heart* and
Homework

WHAT TO READ

WHAT
— TO —
READ

The Essential Guide for
Reading Group Members
and Other Book Lovers

MICKEY PEARLMAN, PH.D.

HarperPerennial
A Division of HarperCollinsPublishers

HarperCollins books may be purchased for educational, business, or sales promotional use. For information please write: Special Markets Department, HarperCollins Publishers, Inc., 10 East 53rd Street, New York, NY 10022.

FIRST EDITION

Designed by Jessica Shatan

Library of Congress Cataloging-in-Publication Data

Pearlman, Mickey.
    What to read : the essential guide for reading group members and other book lovers / by Mickey Pearlman.—1st ed.
      p. cm.
    ISBN 0-06-095061-7
    1. Bibliography—United States—Best books. 2. Group reading—United States. I. Title.
Z1035.9.P4   1994
015.73—dc20   93-44807

95 96 97 98 RRD(H) 10 9 8 7

for Mia and Ted

and in memory of their grandmother,
Anna Pearlman,

and for my friend and Latin teacher, who
died too young, Brother Jerry Markert, Ph.D.:
Requiescat in pace meus amicus bonus.

CONTENTS

ACKNOWLEDGMENTS

When my now-grown daughter was a young girl and I was an academic regularly attending conferences, she used to say, "Don't worry; if you drop my mother out of an airplane and she lands on a college campus or in a bookstore, she'll know somebody." (Fortunately, that theory never had to be tested.) But it became clear in writing this book that no one person, including this one, has read everything, and that input from many other readers (including the ones on those campuses and in those bookstores) would prove invaluable. So many people have helped me that I list their names alphabetically here to protect the innocent from unpopular choices or omissions in the categories to which they paid special attention. For those errors I take full responsibility, and I urge you to use the coupon in the back of the book to let me know which of your favorite books have not been included.

Many thanks to all of you: Kathryn Barkos; Jane Beirn; Carol Benet, Ph.D.; Betsy Bernhard; Michelle Cliff; Sanda Cohen; Lynda B. Daugherty; Robin Diener; Christina Dixcy; Eamon Dolan; Julie Dubuisson; Michael Flamini; Karen Joy Fowler; Lynn Gilbert, Bill Glaser; Lois Gold, Ed.D.; Alexander Gottschalk; Katy Gottschalk, Ph.D.; Sara Gottschalk; Nancy Hellinghausen; Katherine Usher Henderson, Ph.D.; Arlene Hirschfelder; Dennis Hirschfelder; Nora M. Hudson; Kanani Kauka; Donald G. Keller; Burt Kimmelman, Ph.D.; David Kleinman; Julie Kurland; Gloria Williams Ladd; Pearl Laufer, Ph.D.; Betsy Levins; Pat Levinson; Lois Lipton; Margot Livesey; Judy Lowry; Lois Lowry; Jill McCorkle; Margaret L. McDonald, Ph.D.; Jane Taylor McDonnell, Ph.D.; Harriet Marcus; Jim Marks; Katie May; Margaret Meggs; Phyllis Meras; John Meyers; Diane Newman; John Paul; Mia

Pearlman; Ted Pearlman; Nancy Perkins; Elaine Petrocelli; Carl Raymond; Janete Rigg, Ph.D.; Kim Lacy Rogers, Ph.D.; Leslie Rosenzwieg; Roberta Rubin; Helen Ruther; Carla Seaquist; Jill Shanker; Harriet Shapiro; Judi Stern; Dinah Stotler; Mary C. Sturtevant; Deena Stutman; Chip Sullivan, Ph.D.; Mary Rose Sullivan, Ph.D.; Jane von Mehren; Austin Wallace; Karen Warth; Sylvia Watanabe; Abby H. P. Werlock, Ph.D.; Roberta White, Ph.D.; Nancy Willard; Terry Tempest Williams; Wendy Wolf; Buz Wyeth.

Grateful acknowledgment must be given to these librarians in Cliffside Park, New Jersey: Marie Brady, Brian Cazanave, Jane Galgoci, Gloria Hand, Rose Kehoe, Loretta Martinotti, Michele White, and Peggy Wylie. A special thank-you goes to Michele Skowronski, who made the Interlibrary Loan system beg for mercy (and, on my behalf, showed none!). They are all very glad this book is finished.

Finally, I am immensely grateful for my agent, Anne Dubuisson, of the Ellen Levine Literary Agency, who is also a friend and advocate, and for a talented, funny, and hard-working editor, Peternelle van Arsdale.

WHAT TO READ

A NOTE TO THE READER

For the last several years I have been on the road, either talking and listening to writing women—from Jane Smiley and Joyce Carol Oates to Lucille Clifton and Nancy Willard—or speaking at bookstores about the two collections of interviews, *A Voice of One's Own* and *Listen to Their Voices*, for which these conversations were designed.

While this has been a lot of fun, a peculiar phenomenon has emerged both from these experiences and from several stints as a speaker or writer-in-residence at various colleges. During every college seminar or bookstore talk, the news emerges that I have been running a "book club" for several years and that I have an extensive reading list on computer disk. *And talk about interest!* Now I can quickly recognize those shy looks as the students or book buyers approach me and quietly ask if I would mind printing out my reading list so their well-established or newly forming reading group can use it.

This is what writers call a book idea waiting to happen—and you are holding the result in your hands now, greatly augmented from the dozens of lists sent to me from generous reading groups in bookstores, libraries, and homes around the country. A few caveats need to be added, however, about how to approach the thirty-three lists included in *What to Read*. I have tried hard to be inclusive—paying some attention, for example, to ethnicity, in "Mi Vida Latina"; to religion, "A Jewish View"; and to race, "African-American Images and Ideas," "From Asian Shores," and "Native American Literature." (But of course all works by writers of Asian, African, or Native American heritage, or of the Jewish faith, are *not* listed only on those lists—*nor should they be.*)

Geography seems important to me since many, many writers are inspired by place and community, and "Go West," "Southern Comfort," "New York Stories," and "In Caribbean Waters" speak to that phenomenon. The list called "Gay Writes," where writing men and women address the issue of homosexuality in fiction and nonfiction, exists to serve a large and growing audience for these books.

At the same time I have tried to be expansive—including categories that speak more to readers' preferences, like the thousands of mystery novel devotees. Some excellent writing appears on the lists called "The Butler Did it? Unlikely," "War Is Hell . . . Continued," and "One to Beam Up, Mr. Scott," the latter compiled for the prospective or already enthusiastic science fiction reader.

Since a book of this sort inevitably reflects the taste and interests of the writer, I've included a list entitled "Save the Planet," largely books about the physical environment in the United States, since I am outliving many of the trees I have loved. (They are wood pulp.) There are no lists on How to Succeed in Business Even While Trying Very Hard, which interests me not at all. "Be a Sport" (for the armchair or actual athletes among us) does reflect one of my own continuing enthusiasms, although I admit that for me the word "sports" always means baseball. My fascination with the inexplicable is long-standing, so "Questioning the Miraculous" and "Fairy Tales for Grown-ups" (sojourns into the magical and mythical) appear here, but there are no lists on nutrition, fashion, self-help, and none that addresses the mountain of books on technology. If you wish to pursue books on these subjects and you are not familiar with this valuable reference, ask your librarian to introduce you to *Books in Print.*

Since I hope *What to Read* will also serve parents, aunts, and godfathers who are buying books for children, "Kid Stuff" (with forty entries) suggests a basic library of both classics and newer books, mainly for the young adult reader. So many good books for children and young adults exist today that children's departments (17,000 choices in a Nashua, New Hampshire, Barnes & Noble alone) threaten to overtake the entire establishment, and many chains have separate stores. (By the way, children's reading clubs are starting to appear in after-school programs and in bookstores across the country, and recent surveys report that sales of children's books doubled between 1985 and 1991.) All book lovers hope these efforts will help children in our MTV/Nintendo world become good readers, and that they will lighten the burden on teachers—who are now responsible for everything from breakfast and nutrition, AIDS and sex education, to gun control and weapon removal on the playground. (They could use the help.)

Finally, although no one would expect a reading group to spend an entire year, for instance, on "The Impact of Illness," you might want to include one or two books on this subject, and this list lets you choose. On the other hand, I would greatly encourage any reading group to spend a year reading biography, memoir, and autobiography, and to this end there are two lists under the rubric of "Let's Talk About Me": one about the lives of women, one evoking the experiences of men. Many of these speak of family relationships (don't miss "Family Feuds"), and that unending fascination is explored further in "Mothers and Daughters" and in an accompanying list called "Fathers, Sons, and Brothers." Both could have been tripled in length had there been space to do it.

I hope you will keep this guide in your briefcase or bookbag and that you will use it when you visit your local library or bookstore, and when your book club is deciding what to read. And remember what Isaac Asimov said: "Thinking is the activity I love best, and writing to me is simply thinking through my fingers." Reading saves those thoughts and cradles them in the safety of your own welcoming hands.

MICKEY PEARLMAN, PH.D.

INTRODUCTION

So you thought that patchwork quilts, block parties, double-headers, Monday night football; Thanksgiving dinners, Rose Bowl parades, and rodeos were American phenomena. And so they are. But add to this list one of America's best and most productive creations—the reading group.

Book or reading clubs have been going strong since some tired women finally sat down in Charlestown, Massachusetts, around 1813 to read nonfiction. In 1878 the Chautauqua Literary and Scientific Circle, part of the Baptist-affiliated cultural center in western New York State, was organized to send out books—*A Short History of the English People, Fourteen Weeks in Human Physiology, Merivale's General History of Rome, Cyrus the Great and Alexander the Great,* and *Walks and Talks in the Geological Field*—to readers, who were often isolated on farms and in other rural places. According to William Zinsser in *American Places* (New York: HarperCollins, 1992), those members (over 8,400 people in the Chautauqua Circle's first year) would read together in small, hometown discussion groups, and those who completed the four-year course would descend on Chautauqua for a summer graduation ceremony. "Within a decade enrollment had reached 100,000, and by 1914 the program had enlisted half a million members in 12,000 circles in every state and had graduated almost 49,000" (p. 147). Most circles formed in towns of 3,500 people or fewer, mainly in Pennsylvania, Ohio, New York, Iowa, and Illinois, but, says Zinsser, "lively groups also sprang up in big cities such as New York, Brooklyn, Philadelphia and Chicago (p. 147). Sometimes the members (most of whom were women) met "in a Methodist, Presbyterian, Baptist or Episcopalian church; denominational ties were encouraged. . . . They were hungry for the education they hadn't been able to obtain, and some of the most poignant mementos in the club's archives are letters from farm wives, explaining that they had been too busy with their chores to finish the assignment on time" (p. 147).

The Great Books Foundation, a concept promoted by Robert Maynard Hutchins and Mortimer Adler, both of the University of Chicago, was launched in 1947. They published inexpensive editions of selected books (by Plato, Rousseau, Shakespeare, Gibbon, for example); trained leaders in a method called "shared inquiry" (ask but never answer interpretive questions); and encouraged the establishment of book clubs, many of which still exist.

Now reading groups are everywhere, and you certainly don't have to be a Methodist, Presbyterian, Episcopalian, or even a Baptist to join one. (And you are most definitely not limited to the so-called Great Books.) In fact, if you only want to read Victorian novels, African-American writers, fiction by women, American literature, mysteries, biography, award winners—it's easy to find a group that suits your taste. Check at your local library. One of the best is in Elmhurst, Illinois, where the librarians are so organized they issue bookmarks, listing, for example, the "1993 Book Discussions" with the selections, dates of the meetings (starting January 20 with Lee Smith's *Fair and Tender Ladies* and ending on November 17 with Alexandre Dumas's *The Count of Monte Cristo*), their phone number, and the name of the room in which they meet. According to Betsy Levins, head of Adult Services, this group dates back to 1979, and its first book was either *Trinity* by Leon Uris or *Daniel Martin* by John Fowles. There are day and evening sessions, and "*the choice of the book is entirely up to the librarian* [my emphasis] leading the discussions," she adds. Her words tend to make me a little nervous since I still remember what ensued when the southern librarian of my childhood caught me—in the long ago

1950s—reading novels in the Adult Section. (Librarian to my mother: "What's this child doing, reading Faulkner?" Mother to librarian: "She's up to the F's.")

Levins says that the Elmhurst group reads "a healthy mix of classic and contemporary, fiction and nonfiction, U.S. and foreign authors." She herself belongs to the "Adult Reading Round Table," a Chicago group dedicated to advising librarians, that issues its own list of "50 Fiction Titles Used Successfully in Book Discussions"—starting with Richard Adams's *Watership Down* and ending with *The Eighth Day* by Thornton Wilder.

But the enthusiasm for reading groups is not limited to libraries. In Westchester County more than fifty women appeared at Briarcliff Manor's Books N Things after an initial ad ran in a local paper. They eventually broke up into smaller groups of ten to twelve. (At this store, they hold an election of sorts to choose what to read. Anyone who makes a suggestion describes her choice, and then the assembled readers vote.) Book Passage in Corte Madera, California, one of the best bookstores in the country and one deeply committed to reading groups, runs four book clubs of twenty-four members each, for ten-week sessions. All are taught by Carol Bennett, Ph.D., who leads eleven book clubs in that area. And because the interest in reading groups transcends cultural backgrounds, Book Passage now offers sessions in Spanish as well as English.

And don't discount the South. In Knoxville, Tennessee, thirty customers attended a book club "Match-Making Evening" at Davis-Kidd Booksellers, and similar events are arranged in Lexington, Kentucky, at Joseph Beth Bookstore. Or the North: Philadelphia's Borders Book Shop has a packed reading group, and the new Barnes & Noble superstore on New York City's Upper West Side has four free reading groups—women's studies, mysteries, fiction, and African-American writers—which "sold out" four days after they were announced. The discussions, which were planned to last for one hour, often go on for three, and Nancy Hellinghausen, who created all the reading lists, says that participants in the African-American group have gone on to visit the Schomburg Center for Black History in Harlem and to have dinner together.

Bookstores like the famed Politics & Prose in downtown Washington, D.C., sponsor public reading clubs every month except August with groups of twelve to thirty-five readers who concentrate on fiction by authors abroad, often published by small presses. (They discuss the choices, but Carla Cohen, the owner, has the final say!) Chapters, another great Washington bookstore, runs a poetry group that discusses new collections; their meetings are planned to coincide with visits of poets to the store. In Winnetka, Illinois, Roberta Rubin says that since 1985 she and her staff have been sending out 3,000 "book list/invitations" for their "Wednesday Mornings at The Book Stall at Chestnut Court," where book discussion leaders, adult education experts, writers, and Ph.D. candidates lead discussions on everything from Tolstoy's *The Death of Ivan Ilyich* to "*Presumed Innocent* and *Burden of Proof*: a study of Scott Turow's books." Like most stores, it has a "hardcore group of twenty or so and then new people each time," says Rubin. She adds that since the spring of 1993 there has been "one new wrinkle—a five-dollar charge that entitles you to a five-dollar merchandise coupon."

Does all this sound as if book discussion groups bring in business and that bookstores are crazy about them? You bet. And even when reading groups do not meet there, they often provide advice, as Denver's Tattered Cover has done for more than 125 reading clubs in that city, up from fifty only two or three years ago.

Other reading groups have evolved from professional affiliations, like the club in Winston-Salem, North Carolina, consisting mostly of faculty and medical school employees at Wake Forest Medical School. They admit that "about half of the meeting is social," and like most reading groups they meet in various living rooms. (Some groups use places of worship.)

Many groups are mixed by gender, age, and education, or

share a heritage, like the club at a New York City synagogue where several pairs of married couples argue regularly. I was one of their guest leaders and taught a so-called woman's book (their translation: a novel *by a woman*), which was scheduled, unfortunately, for the day after a Pro-Choice March on Washington with which certain members were unhappy. I'm happy to say that my wounds have healed nicely and that I did not require reconstructive surgery. Some groups, like "Monday Night Readers" of Columbia, Maryland, and "Belles Lettres" of Short Hills, New Jersey, are restricted to women, but of varying races and/or religions. All have members who note that their taste in literature has evolved along with their careers, and many believe that their intensified sense of their own potential is related in still-unexplained ways to their reading experience.

Clearly, we are in a time when trendy phrases like "saloning" and "cocooning" reflect a deep need to connect with each other. Many people are choosing to trade in the scramble for riches, exemplified by the last several decades, for an experience that is, instead, enriching. Reading groups are here to stay. My own mother, who had been a member of the "Books in Brief Bookclub of Miami, Florida" for thirty years—when she died at eighty-six—would be pleased.

HOW TO ORGANIZE

It's not necesssary to reinvent the wheel. If you are thinking of organizing a reading group, here's how other clubs did it and what they think works.

A Bite out of Books in the Big Apple

According to Lynn Gilbert, all the members of her New York City book club ("including the teacher, who is paid and is as much a member as a leader) come with credentials: one was a college valedictorian, another is a writer, and they all have great language skills. *Choose your members not by how many books they have read but by what they read.* And invite them to sit in for a meeting before they are asked to join. That way you get an idea of what kinds of questions they will ask."

Gilbert says that you need at least fourteen members (in her group they range in age from twenty-six to sixty), "with a minimum of nine, to make it work, even though we have no problems with members not showing up. In fact, one member, who was gong to veterinary school in Pennsylvania, came home each month for the meeting."

Gilbert's club is one of seven that was chosen by the publisher of Sue Miller's *For Love* for a trendsetting visit by that author several years ago. The desire of publishers and bookstores to court reading groups is now so great that *if you call the publicity department of any major publisher, and you live in any of the cities where the author is appearing at book-*

stores, you may be able to arrange a visit by one of your favorite writers.

New Jersey Book Lovers

The Garden State has the best reading groups in the country. (Okay, I'm from New Jersey.) And my own reading group, "The Bones-in-a-Baggie Book Club," is still flourishing after eight years! (About the name: well, during one particularly memorable discussion, a member did tell this v-e-r-y l-o-n-g story about a friend whose husband was cremated, but when they sent the ashes north . . .)

Many of the original members still attend, with one loyalist now commuting, when possible, from Boston. The biggest change over the years is that almost without exception, all the women now work. The new members—a lawyer, a science teacher, a garment center executive, a learning deficiency expert—all add grandly to the mix, which already included two sculptors, a science teacher, a business supplies executive, a certified public accountant, and several teachers.

This group meets in members' homes for eight sessions per year, the last one of the year always taking place, with dinner, in the leader's apartment. She chooses the books, and when we do the classics—*Middlemarch, Anna Karenina, Frankenstein*—the longest books are always assigned at the last meeting of the year for reading over the summer. We often read fiction by women in which concepts of space are important (we've noticed all those depressed females sitting, and crying, in closets) and novels with political and social undertones (i.e., incest, fragmented families, missing mothers). Hospital's *The Last Magician*, Coetzee's *Waiting for the Barbarians, Forms of Shelter* by Angela Davis-Gardner, Rosellen Brown's *Before and After*, and Paul Auster's *Moon Palace* have been successful for us. Gail Godwin's *Father Melancholy's Daughter* and Lois Lowry's *The Giver* were particular favorites of many members and elicited discussion about parents and children, individual freedom, abandonment, and betrayal—subjects in which we remain extremely interested.

Like many members of reading groups across the country to whom I have spoken, these readers are devoted to their book club, often postponing anniversary and birthday dinners if they fall on "book club night." They have also become noticeably closer to each other, more tolerant of dissent, and more responsible for their own close, attentive readings of the books. As one of the charter members says, "I'm spoiled now. I can't read trash anymore, not even on the beach. Once you've been touched by the magic of great writing, you can't read the other stuff."

The Maine Event

"The Wayne-Winthrop Women's Reading Group" is so successful, says Mary C. Sturtevant, that although it uses a handout giving the date, place, time, and a short synopsis of the book to be discussed, "we don't have to call anyone—they remember on their own!"

Gloria Williams Ladd, who functions as archivist for the group, explains its genesis: "Two years ago the librarian in our small town arranged through the Maine State Library and the Maine Humanities Council for a reading series: 'The Journey Inward: Women's Autobiographies.' The books and speakers attracted an audience of twenty-five to thirty women and prompted animated discussions about both the nature of autobiography and the personalities of the authors. We enjoyed one another's company so much that we thought we would try to conduct the group without the benefit of a leader or speaker." Ladd says they soon realized that "there were decisions to make: *how often and where to meet, what to read, and how to obtain the books.* [So] every two or three months we plan ahead for the next several meetings [because it] does require some organization to keep . . . functioning. We *do* have a self-appointed leader/facilitator who types up the meeting schedule, arranges for an occasional speaker, and *orders the books in advance from a local bookseller or remainder catalog.* [*Edward Hamilton* or *Daedalus* are two such catalogs; the addresses are available in any library.] Twenty women looking for the same book from a small-town library or from interlibrary loan would overload our system, so our *librarian supports us by having one available copy of our monthly selection.* Our local *independent bookstore has offered us a 15 percent discount* on our orders and usually stocks a copy or two of the books we read. The leader/facilitator prefaces each discussion with a brief biography of the author and a summary of the work." (For such background information, refer to *Contemporary Literary Criticism* and *Contemporary Authors*, both published by Gale Research, and the *Dictionary of Literary Biography.*)

This group consists of women ranging in age from the midtwenties to midseventies. According to Ladd, the retirees "read more and longer books than some of our younger members, who have jobs and children." *Most groups profit from this mix.* "We have found that meeting once a month from 7:00 P.M. to 9:00 P.M. works well for us all; it allows us to read something other than the chosen book, to take care of our families, and to pursue other pleasures. Two years later, we are still reading 'women authors,' though not necessarily autobiographies, but our discussions still flow from members' concerns and reflections. Women who enjoy reading will always find a theme, a character, or a relationship they would like to explore with others. . . . The important thing is that we don't need an expert or a critic to tell us what to think about an author or book. It's our opinions, and insights, that are important to us. All it takes is a group of women who want to share their experiences and a little organization. The books are out there waiting."

Reading at a University in Tennessee

Think about meeting at a college or university in your area. Why? At "The Women's Center Book Group" at Vanderbilt University in Nashville, organized in 1986, one member (who works in the library) includes the individual book orders of group members with her regular orders to the distributor. (Members sign up for the next *two* books to be ordered.) This means that reading group members get a 20 percent discount on paperback and 40 percent off on hardcover books. The next month's book is sent through campus mail or picked up at the Women's Center, which also provides clerical support—sending out the schedule after they choose books, coordinating changes in the order, and keeping the membership/mailing list updated. The Center also supplies coffee, tea, and juice, *and* microwave popcorn and cookies!

This Nashville group meets throughout the year on the second Monday of each month from 5:15 P.M. to 6:15 P.M., and although the group is campus-based, about half of the regular membership is not affiliated with Vanderbilt. *Every six to eight months the members choose the books for the next six to eight months*, and at the same time individual members agree to facilitate particular discussions.

Margaret L. Meggs, assistant to the director of the Women's Studies Program, says that they "agreed at the organization of the group, and have reconfirmed this all along, to be a women-only group, and unless there's a significant reason to do otherwise, to read books written by women. We try to be broad-based in our selections, with attention to classics and recent publications, fiction and nonfiction, and to honor cultural/racial/other diversity. We read well-known and obscure writers, and books by speakers who may be appearing on campus. However, every December our selection is a mystery novel, and we have great fun with it, usually making the meeting a festive occasion for whichever holidays members celebrate." As Meggs says, "Usually all the leader has to do is give a bit of info and ask a question, and we're off."

On the Potomac

This group of eighteen "mostly Washington lawyers" is so successful, says its archivist, Carla Seaquist, a writer and playwright, that in November of 1989 they gave themselves a "tenth anniversary champagne bash" at the home of a member of President Clinton's cabinet. (For the same meeting they read Melville's *Billy Budd*.) As you would expect, Seaquist adds, they do plenty of arguing about what to read, but when they do choose, it is clear that these readers are not kidding around. Theirs is the only list I have seen that includes *The Iliad*, Dante's *Inferno*, Gogol's *Dead Souls*, Camus's *The Plague*, and, on *one* night—*Dr. Jekyll and Mr. Hyde, Frankenstein*, and "Monkey's Paw" by W. W. Jacobs. Back in 1985, when they were still warming up, they attended *Othello* at the Folger, had supper at a restaurant in D.C., and in the same month read Woolf's *Mrs. Dalloway* (296 pages) and *Cranford* (244 pages) by Elizabeth Gaskell. In 1991 they read Balzac's *Père Goriot* and attended the Folger production of *King Lear*. Apparently that energized them for the 1992 reading schedule which lists, all in June, Updike's "*Rabbit Run* (extra credit: *Rabbit Redux*) and *Rabbit at Rest* (extra credit: *Rabbit Is Rich*)."

In 1993 they're doing the easy stuff: Fontane's *Effi Brest*, Trevor's *Two Lives, Palace Walk* by Mahfouz, *In the Skin of the Lion* by Michael Ondaatje, *Bastard Out of Carolina* by Dorothy Allison, *The Man of Property* by John Galsworthy, *Outerbridge Reach* by Robert Stone, and Trollope's *Phineas Finn*.

Whew! And Bravo.

African-American Readers in Detroit

Attorney-at-law Nora Hudson describes her "Woman's Cultural Club/Literary Circle" as women "with similar ideas who get together to engage in useful purposes . . . The recipe for a successful book club is like any other: you need the right ingredients—a few persons with a sense of humor who enjoy networking, a few persons who are looking for support, and a few persons who are chronic complainers; in other words, a variety of viewpoints." According to Hudson, this club "grew out of a need to alleviate the stress and strain of being working wives or single parents, and the core group consisted of women who were old college friends." When they got together for birthdays and Christmas, she says, they often talked "about their need to have time alone with friends with the same interests in cultural activities, literature, poetry, and creative writing," and even before their club was organized they would share books, inform each other of local cultural events, and often attend as a group. One of them always hosted the "night of beauty, or a Christmas Sing-along, Christmas or spring brunch, trip to the Art Institute or Stratford Festival, block picnic for the kids, or the sale of tickets to church events." As Hudson explains, because "we all belonged to too many formal organizations with bylaws, officers, dues, and rules or regulations—which added stress—[we decided that] this club would have none. We just agreed to meet, and members volunteered to be in charge of monthly meetings." (She notes that many clubs do decide to incorporate or register with their counties, or to charge dues to defray postage or other expenses.)

For the sake of order, they have now decided to prepare a six-month schedule of monthly coordinators and a book list. (*Such planning is both necessary and inevitable if a reading club is to work.*) The coordinator is responsible for choosing the author, investigating his or her oeuvre, notifying the group members of the date of the meeting (scheduled for the third or fourth Sunday of the month, from 3:00 P.M. to 6:00 P.M., because most members attend church on Sunday mornings on a regular basis), and for selecting the location.

After *Essence* published a short piece about her club, Hudson says she "received over a hundred calls from interested people all over the country. Fifty-nine people attended our May 1993 new members' meeting, and although we had used members' homes when we had only twenty members, we selected a Mini Health Care Mall and Holistic Center as a meeting place. The rent was fifty dollars for three hours, but the owner was so impressed with our group that he suggested that we take up a collection at the meeting, and he would accept whatever it was, or would even let us have the room for free." (*If you need a meeting place, you can also get in touch with your local independent bookstore.*)

Hudson adds that "if the monthly coordinator opts for an event instead of a discussion, she is responsible for all ticketing information and for the collection of monies." (They must have good coordinators because this group engages in numerous cultural activities: attending Brunch with Bach, *Daughters of the Dust*, and *Black Orpheus*.) The month's coordinator is also responsible for "the repast, which ranges from potluck to potato chips to formal brunches and dinners— whatever she or her budget allows."

Phoenix Rising: Denver

Although I assumed initially that "The Phoenix Book Club" of Denver must have been organized, disbanded, and reorganized, hence the ash-covered bird, Professor Margaret McDonald of the University of Colorado assured me that it was named instead for the first book read by the group: *I Knew a Phoenix* by May Sarton. "They liked her work so much that they chose the name from her title."

McDonald reports that the "doyenne of our all-woman group is a seventy-eight-year-old psychiatrist; we limit the membership to twelve, with four women in each age group: fifties, sixties, and seventies. (The youngest member is forty-nine.) The books, mostly fiction, are picked by the group in August at a retreat in the mountains. [What a great idea!] Each member is asked to make a list of three suggestions, and then the group votes."

Very few contemporary authors appear on their list (García Márquez is an exception) because this club exists to encourage the reading of books forgotten since college or missed completely. Members sometimes read plays, like *Hedda Gabler* and *Tartuffe*, that are being performed at the Denver Center Theater Company, and attend the productions as a group.

McDonald explains that her book club includes several Episcopalians and Congregationalists, some of whom are "disaffected churchgoers," and that their "comparatively mild disagreements" usually involve religion. *The Bridge of San Luis Rey* by Thornton Wilder, says McDonald, "engendered some caustic remarks about superstition in the Roman Catholic Church. Several members then related their own horror stories about unhappy Catholic girlhoods."

Even in the Rockies, a good book heats things up!

Long Winters in Minnesota

Katherine Baker says that her reading club in Northfield—home of St. Olaf College and Carleton College—started as a neighborhood enterprise: "Called, imaginatively, 'The Fourth Thursday Group,' it began with four very close friends, women ranging in age from thirty to forty-three, and has now expanded to include eleven people." Northfield likes book clubs: one has been in existence for more than thirty years, and four more were recently started by the local library. Baker's group meets once a month, at a different person's house, on a rotating basis. The host selects the book and also leads the discussion, although she talks over the choice with members at the previous month's meeting. "The group does have some influence on the choice, but since we've been together for three years we know what each other reads, and can easily choose books that no one in the group has read—usually fiction, with some nonfiction thrown in now and again." (Their list includes, as you would expect in Minnesota, with its profusion of Scandinavian ancestors, Rolvaag's *Giants in the Earth*, but also *Antigone* and *Fried Green Tomatoes at the Whistle Stop Cafe.*) The host provides "some historical background or a newspaper article on the author or subject, or a videotape of the author discussing the book. But we try to *save the author's comments until after we have discussed the book* because we want to explore it by ourselves first. Then it is fun to see how well we understood what the author was trying to achieve. This was especially helpful with Doris Lessing's *The Fifth Child*. Since we live in a town with two colleges, we are sometimes able to have experts come and talk to us. We did this with Rushdie's *Satanic Verses*; a professor came and talked to us about the religions of India and Pakistan." An English professor was on hand for Erdrich's *The Beet Queen*. (This is a fine idea, and with 3,000 colleges and universities in the United States, a professor should not be far from your living room, bookstore, or library. You might think about inviting these guests to bring along their own books, which they could then talk about and sell.)

Baker says they "did not set out to be an all-women group; they evolved into it." The only problem, she notes, is that "we are all too close in age to have vastly different reactions to images and ideas." But nobody, she adds, is dropping out.

Northwest Territory

Dinah Stotler's book club in Seattle has no name, but it *was* one of the reading groups visited by Sue Miller, "who fit right in and was right at home!" This club dates from 1973, and its original members, now in their late forties and early fifties, were friends at the University of Washington. (If you are looking for members, try your alumni/alumnae bulletin.) There are still some members "at home, waiting for the kids to go off to college," but most are writers, artists, accountants, and even house renovators.

Stotler says her group is "loosely organized but someone does usually volunteer to get reviews of the book and to be the leader." Members try to "stick to paperbacks" because they are all prodigious readers and "it gets expensive." The group has spent some time worrying about whether, for instance, they have "done too many southern writers so they recently spent a year reading British fiction. They've also read Charles Johnson's *Middle Passage*, since this writer teaches in their part of the country, and recently discussed the 1949 award-winning *Bridge on the Drina*. That choice was inspired by a member who works for the Red Cross and spent four weeks in Bosnia. Once a year they meet at Elliot Bay Bookstore, one of the best in the country, where a staff person advises them on what is new and makes suggestions. *This is a good idea for all reading groups without a paid teacher because almost all decent bookstores now have people who can advise you.*

Stotler adds that they are thinking of moving their meeting time to an early 6:00 P.M. (skipping the desserts and adding wine), so they can "get home, get to sleep, and get up for work the next day."

Reading Jewish Writers in California

Carol Benet, Ph.D., the reigning reading group queen of northern California (she teaches eleven of them!), leads this group of eighteen married and single men and women, which includes heart surgeons, psychiatrists, and poets. They read only works by Jewish writers. (The members are not necessarily Jewish.) It grew out of the Bronfman Seminars, sponsored by the University of California six years ago.

The aim here is to read the most representative books of the Jewish experience—in each decade from the 1890s to the present—and then to relax, after five months of discussion, with a potluck at a member's home.

Benet is a great believer in reading lists built around a theme, especially when (as is the case here) the members of a club are "not really friends, but were brought together through the books." Her group, for instance, has read Arthur Hertzberg's *Jews in America*, Sholem Asch's *East River*, *Call It Sleep* by Henry Roth, the play *Waiting for Lefty* by Clifford Odets, Alfred Kazin's *A Walker in the City*, Bernard Malamud's *A New Life*, Rosellen Brown's *Civil Wars*, and Abraham Cahan's *The Rise of David Levinsky*. Members have also read Arthur Miller's *Death of a Salesman* and watched the Dustin Hoffman version on video.

Benet offered some other good ideas: think about a year of

reading National Book Award or Booker Prize winners, or Nobel laureates. If you live in an area where writers lived, or about which they wrote, visit the sites described in the novels. (She takes one of her groups to John's Grill, where the action in Dashiell Hammett's *Maltese Falcon* takes place, and to the Sonoma site where Jack London's house burned down before he could move in.) My guess is that you will find restaurants and bookstores in these areas eager to help you.

California Dreamers? Not in this group.

In addition to all the good advice offered by these ten reading groups, I would like to add the following suggestions and comments:

• Although some may disagree, I strongly advocate hiring a teacher/leader for any reading group, even if you choose to keep the selection of *what to read* in members' hands. No group is so far from a good high school English teacher, or an underpaid college professor, that this option should prove impossible. It is clear from my conversations with dozens of reading group members that time must be found—first to read and then to attend a reading group. Very little is left to research reviews or valid criticism or to construct a thoughtful and probing direction for the discussion. These tasks should be the responsibility of a teacher who is already trained not only to provide answers but to supply the right questions.

• Ban at the outset any discussion that focuses on, "Did you like the book?" This is not a popularity contest, and any worthwhile piece of fiction, no matter how beloved or detested, teaches the reader something. The real issue is the choice of what to read.

• If your reading group is also a social occasion, set specific times for book discussion that are not encroached upon by other conversation.

• Choose one person to arbitrate disagreements and conflicts during the discussion, especially if you do not hire a teacher.

• Try to establish at the outset that you expect all members to attend all sessions, except for emergencies, business trips, and family obligations that cannot be postponed. A reading group (like any other organization) creates its own dynamic, which is seriously disturbed when the configuration (in this case, people) changes.

• Have fun. There is no midterm or term paper, and there will be *no* pop quizzes!

1

FAMILY FEUDS

1. *Shadow Play*   **Charles Baxter**
Multilayered novel of life in Five Oaks, Michigan, where love
and social responsibility collide. Beautifully written, almost
melodic, with a clear moral vision (as is *First Light*, his first
novel).   **352 pp.; 1993**

2. *Mystery Ride*   **Robert Boswell**
The mystery ride in this novel is marriage. (The title is from a
Bruce Springsteen song.) Boswell returns here to his best
material, dysfunctional families, found also in his memorable
second novel, *Crooked Hearts*, set in Yuma, Arizona.
                                                 333 pp.; 1993

3. *The Runaway Soul*   **Harold Brodkey**
Set in the 1930s, this is the story of Wiley Silenowics, an
adopted child who is raised in the household of his cousins
and their daughter, Nonie. Many years in the writing.
                                                 848 pp.; 1993

4. *Before and After*   **Rosellen Brown**
When a New Hampshire teenager kills his girlfriend, his parents are forced to examine their own moral truths as well as
their relationship. A gripping, beautifully written novel.
                                                 354 pp.; 1992

5. *My Antonia* Willa Cather

Turn-of-the-century farm life as lived by Slavic and Scandinavian immigrants on the open prairies of Nebraska and the finest work by one of America's greatest writers. Shimerda emerges from this novel as the most memorable American mother in twentieth-century literature.   372 pp.; 1919

6. *The Beans of Egypt, Maine* Carolyn Chute

The grotesque and the normal come together here and in its successor, *Letourneau's Used Auto Body Parts*. This is life below the poverty line. To quote Chute's publisher, Egypt, Maine, is "a kingdom of blood and dirt and sweat and sperm."   244 pp.; 1984

7. *Mrs. Bridge* Evan Connell

If you've seen the movie, you'll always picture Joanne Woodward in this sympathetic portrayal of a housewife and mother of three in Kansas City between the two world wars. Of course, in the *movie*, Mr. Bridge was Paul Newman, so how bad could things have been?   254 pp.; 1959

8. *Ragtime* E. L. Doctorow

The bestselling story of immigrant Jews on the lower East Side of New York and their evolution into citizens with money and stature. Doctorow is one of America's best writers.   236 pp.; 1975

9. *Geek Love* Katherine Dunn

Olympia Binewski, an albino hunchback dwarf, narrates this novel about her carnival family; will they breed specimens for their own freak show?   348 pp.; 1989

10. *Middlemarch* George Eliot

Considered to be Eliot's masterpiece and one of the greatest books of the nineteenth century, this novel is about life in a provincial English town. The players are Dorothea, a modern St. Teresa; Lyngate, prototype for today's fashionable liposuction doctor; Rosamond, representing triviality and egoism;

and the doomed banker Bulstrode. There is also Casaubon, the husband nobody wants but everyone will recognize. Thoroughly contemporary, and no one is educated without reading it. A must.   **795 pp.; 1871–1872**

11. *Love Medicine*   **Louise Erdrich**
First book in a Native American tetralogy that includes *The Beet Queen, Tracks*, and *The Bingo Palace*, this is the multi-generational story of two families, the Kashpaws and the Lamartines.   **304 pp.; 1984**

12. *The Sound and the Fury*   **William Faulkner**
Difficult but compelling study of the Compsons, an old southern family. This novel concentrates on that complex and subtle time of memory that meshes past and present, reality and illusion, the conscious and the subconscious. My personal choice for best American novel written in the first half of this century. Demanding but more than worth it. Read the shorter *As I Lay Dying* too.   **427 pp.; 1929**

13. *Are You Mine?*   **Abby Frucht**
In her third novel Frucht sketches the moral dilemmas brought on by an unexpected third pregnancy. Her power is in humor.   **304 pp.; 1993**

14. *Turtle Moon*   **Alice Hoffman**
A novel about a single mother, her complicated son, and a policeman with guilt.   **255 pp.; 1992**

15. *Natural History*   **Maureen Howard**
When a society tramp kills a soldier toward the end of World War II, Billy Bray, a detective, is called on to investigate the case. The murder reveals an undertow of sex, crime, and moral confusion that sweeps Bray and his family into an uncertain future.   **416 pp.; 1992**

16. *The 14 Sisters of Emilio*   **Oscar Hijuelos**
     Montez O'Brien
The author of the Pulitzer Prize–winning *The Mambo Kings*

Play Songs of Love writes here about an Irish immigrant who travels to Cuba as a photographer during the Spanish-American War and meets the sensitive and poetic Mariela Montez. She bears him fourteen daughters and, finally, a son, Emilio. A paean to the feminine from a male author.   **484 pp.; 1993**

17. *Very Old Bones*   William Kennedy
By the author of *Ironweed*, this sixth novel is a fictionalized version of Kennedy's life as a writer. Albany is for him what Dublin was for Joyce.   **292 pp.; 1992**

18. *Passing On*   Penelope Lively
A Booker Prize winner in 1987 for *Moon Tiger* writes about the death of a difficult mother and follows the lives of her middle-aged son and daughter.   **224 pp.; 1992**

19. *Learning By Heart*   Margot Livesey
A collection of stories about the connections people make or, in most cases, fail to make. The title story about a girl and her stepmother is particularly important. Livesey also wrote *Homework*, a novel.   **248 pp.; 1986**

20. *The Member of the Wedding*   Carson McCullers
McCullers, who died young, was only twenty-three when she created a literary sensation with this novel. Frankie Addams, a twelve-year-old girl, jealous of her brother's marriage, dresses up as F. Jasmaine, meets up with a serviceman, and makes other plans.   **195 pp.; 1946**

21. *At Weddings and Wakes*   Alice McDermott
The tender and captivating story of an Irish-American family in Brooklyn during the 1950s and 1960s, and their encounters with ordinary rituals and extraordinary emotions. *That Night* is good too.   **213 pp.; 1992**

22. *Long Day's Journey into Night*   Eugene O'Neill
A play that catalogs the ills of America's dysfunctional families: drug addiction, alcoholism, disaffected children, jealousy among siblings, bad marriages, etc. In the Tyrones we see the entire list.   **176 pp.; 1956**

23. *A Suitable Boy*   Vikram Seth
Set in India at the beginning of its independence, this is the
very long (but interesting) story of four large extended families in a time of upheaval. Seth also wrote a 1986 novel in
verse, *The Golden Gate*.   1,349 pp.; 1993

24. *A Thousand Acres*   Jane Smiley
A modern version of King Lear and his daughters, this time
on an Iowa farm, but with the additional burden of incest.
The book won both the Pulitzer Prize and National Book
Award for 1991. Also recommended is *Ordinary Love and
Good Will*, two novellas.   371 pp.; 1991

25. *The Man Who Loved Children*   Christina Stead
This masterpiece by a third-generation Australian is about a
father, six children, a stepchild, and a mother named Henny,
who, as Randall Jarrell wrote, is "one of those immortal
beings in whom the tragedy of existence is embodied."
                                                    491 pp.; 1940

26. *The Kitchen God's Wife*   Amy Tan
In the story that the Chinese mother Winnie tells her American daughter, Pearl, another family emerges. A novel about
secrets, class differences (particularly in China), and the ways
in which male-dominated cultures operate, it follows *The Joy
Luck Club*, her astounding literary debut. Again Tan creates
an unforgettable, multifaceted mother.   415 pp.; 1991

27. *Saint Maybe*   Anne Tyler
Tyler is America's chief chronicler of domesticity and its dis-
contents, often in Baltimore. Here Ian Bedloe, seventeen,
stumbles into a storefront that houses the Church of the Second Chance, a tiny popular sect that demands reparations
from its members for their sins.   337 pp.; 1991

28. *To the Lighthouse*   Virginia Woolf
The chief figure of modernism in England writes about the
Ramsay family, their artistic friend Lily Briscoe, and how the
trifling events of everyday existence define life. If you are
interested in symbols, this is your book!   310 pp.; 1927

2

EVIL LURKS

1. *Bastard Out of Carolina*   **Dorothy Allison**
Ruth Anne Boatwright, the teenage daughter of a luckless, southern, "white trash" woman, suffers sexual abuse from her vicious stepfather in South Carolina. Rooted in autobiography, as is her short story collection, *Trash*.   309 pp.; 1992

2. *Affliction*   **Russell Banks**
Wade Whitehouse, a part-time policeman, is the poster child for male violence. In the struggle between decency and brutality, Whitehouse represents a man beset by the dark side of the macho mentality.   355 pp.; 1989

3. *Violence*   **Richard Bausch**
Public and private forms of brutality, including an armed robbery, dominate this masterly novel by a very fine contemporary writer.   293 pp.; 1992

4. *Meeting Evil*   **Thomas Berger**
Evil shows up this time in the person of Richie, a cheerful psychopath standing in John Felton's doorway. 256 pp.; 1992

5. *A Clockwork Orange*   **Anthony Burgess**
Alex, a vicious fifteen-year-old hoodlum, is the central character in this thirty-year-old book, a nightmare vision of the future. This is a frightening fable about good and evil, and, if

you read the newspaper, you will see that a lot of it sounds eerily familiar. **192 pp.; 1962**

6. *In Cold Blood* **Truman Capote**
One of the first "nonfiction novels." In this terrifying portrayal of the brutal mass murder by two psychopaths of an entire family, the Clutters, Capote captures an event that now seems horrifyingly familiar, and not just in Kansas.

343 pp.; 1965

7. *Falconer* **John Cheever**
After the death of his brother, a college professor named Ezekiel Farragut ends up an unlikely convict in cellblock A, in a prison called Falconer. Cheever's best work. **226 pp.; 1977**

8. *Waiting for the Barbarians* **J. M. Coetzee**
This second prize-winning novel by the South African writer is an allegory of the war between the oppressor and the oppressed. Here it is the Magistrate who lives in complicity with the Empire, a regime he comes to deplore. **156 pp.; 1981**

9. *Heart of Darkness* **Joseph Conrad**
The story of Marlow, Conrad's famous maritime wanderer in Africa, and how he first hears the name Kurtz ("He dead"), the elusive figure at the heart of darkness. **117 pp.; 1902**

10. *Deliverance* **James Dickey**
Four men set out from a small southern town for a three-day camping and canoe trip. What they find is murder, sexual violence, and the violence of nature. Even better than the movie, which was actually quite good. **239 pp.; 1970**

11. *Play It As It Lays* **Joan Didion**
Loveless sex, drugs, violence, and booze in a grim portrayal of a California world where people use each other without sympathy or conscience. **214 pp.; 1989**

12. *Lord of the Flies* **William Golding**
Golding won the Nobel Prize for literature in 1983 although this book was first published almost thirty years earlier. Proper British schoolboys are marooned on a deserted island,

and the struggle between good and evil begins. Evil wins.

243 pp.; 1954

13. *The Firm*   **John Grisham**
When Mitch McDeere, a *supposed* genius graduate of Harvard Law, is offered a BMW, house, and eighty grand a year by a Memphis law firm in the 1980s, his suspicions should have been raised; you would have had to be lobotomized not to see the Mafia behind the scenes in this one.   **501 pp.; 1991**

14. *Dogeaters*   **Jessica Hagedorn**
Nominated for a National Book Award, Hagedorn's story describes a Philippines where Hollywood dreams and tropical nightmares violently collide. Wonderfully developed characters—from young junkies to feisty schoolgirls.   **251 pp.; 1990**

15. *Damage*   **Josephine Hart**
Father and son are both sexually involved with a dangerous, damaging, tall, and usually black-garbed, woman.

216 pp.; 1991

16. *Seventh Heaven*   **Alice Hoffman**
When Nora Silk arrives in a typical suburban community in the 1950s, everyone asks questions—of her and of themselves. In other words, they think she's a witch. Sound familiar?   **256 pp.; 1990**

17. *The Remains of the Day*   **Kazuo Ishiguro**
Stevens, a model British butler in the last days of the Empire, is the cloth through whom Ishiguro weaves important questions about personality, class, culture, anti-Semitism, and the buried life.   **245 pp.; 1989**

18. *The Night Manager*   **John le Carré**
No more Soviet Union and no more superspy Karla, so le Carré creates an arms-deal-cum-drug-lord named Roper, arrogant and stylish, who rivals the Devil in evil.

429 pp.; 1993

19. *The Fifth Child*   **Doris Lessing**
Contentment reigns in the Lovatt household in 1960s En-

gland until their gruesome, insatiable, hungry, demanding, and violent fifth child arrives. A must by the author of the *Children of Violence* series and *The Golden Notebook*. In my view, her novella, *To Room Nineteen*, is the best thing Lessing ever wrote. **133 pp.; 1988**

20. *Butcher Boy* **Patrick McCabe**
Entering the deranged mind of an Irish schoolboy is not pleasant. Not for the fainthearted. **215 pp.; 1993**

21. *Remembering Babylon* **David Malouf**
In nineteenth-century Queensland, Australia, the dark passions of racism, brutality, and hate surface when Gemmy Fairley, "a British object," emerges from sixteen years of living with the aborigines in the wilderness. **202 pp.; 1993**

22. *Billy Budd, Foretopman* **Herman Melville**
Remember Captain Vere? Innocent Billy is doomed in this seafaring drama because his goodness just might subvert evil. Amazing how a story written in the 1800s can be so modern.
95 pp.; 1924

23. *Homeboy* **Seth Morgan**
Savagely comic and brilliant first novel about the teeming San Francisco netherworld of junkies, pimps, drag queens, and hookers. **400 pp.; 1990**

24. *A Dangerous Woman* **Mary McGarry Morris**
A Vermont loony, Martha Horgan, is not the village saint, but her unspecified derangement takes the form of compulsive honesty. **358 pp.; 1991**

25. *Lolita* **Vladimir Nabokov**
The famous and controversial bestselling novel about Humbert Humbert, a "White Widowed Male," and a seductive twelve-year-old girl. It was shocking then, and it's shocking now. **319 pp.; 1955**

26. *The Rise of Life on Earth* **Joyce Carol Oates**
This short novel sketches Kathleen's violent childhood,

including a broken home, child beating, and murder. Her later exploitation by a young doctor energizes latent fury.

135 pp.; 1991

27. *Yonnondio* Tillie Olsen

Unfinished story of the Holbrook family as they migrate from coal-mining town to farm to industrial slum, set in the depression era of the 1930s; this is a lesson in how an inequitable society destroys the spirit. 133 pp.; 1974

28. *Looking for Mr. Goodbar* Judith Rossner

Tery Dunn, a young schoolteacher, finds more than she wants, including murder, in the Big Apple on New Year's Eve. Remember that this was written many, many years before the infamous Levin case in Central Park. Rossner also wrote *August* and *His Little Women*. 284 pp.; 1975

29. *The Jungle* Upton Sinclair

This muckraking exposé of Chicago's meat-packing industry led directly to the passage of the Pure Food and Drug Act. Only for vegetarians, or those who never plan to eat another hotdog. 346 pp.; 1906

30. *God's Snake* Irini Spanidou

Fearless, passionate first novel about a brave little Greek girl, her authoritarian father, a fragile and wounded mother, and with all the simplicity and power of a Greek myth. Don't miss it. 252 pp.; 1986

31. *Loitering With Intent* Muriel Spark

When the young writer Fleur Talbot becomes the secretary to the Autobiographical Association (whose members are writing their memoirs), she runs into a con artist named Quentin Oliver, the defrocked Father Delaney, among others. In *The Prime of Miss Jean Brodie*, Spark's most famous novel, the unforgettable teacher fails to see the evil that Mussolini represents. 217 pp.; 1981

32. *Perfume* Patrick Süskind

In 1738 Paris a baby is born under a fishmonger's table and

then abandoned. Although this kid has no aroma of his own, he possesses an absolute sense of smell, and his obsession, to isolate the most perfect scent of all, leads to disaster.

255 pp.; 1986

33. *The Secret History* — Donna Tartt
Debut novel about an inner circle of five gifted students at a small Vermont college and the crime they commit.

524 pp.; 1992

3

FAIRY TALES FOR GROWN-UPS

1. *Don Quixote, Which Was A Dream*   Kathy Acker
A feminist retelling of Cervantes's famous tale. **207 pp.; 1986**

2. *The Robber Bride*   Margaret Atwood
The title comes from the Grimm fairy tale about the robber
bridegroom who cuts up and eats his kidnapped maidens.
Here the very malevolent Zenia carries off her three friends'
husbands and boyfriends. She is the ultimate nemesis.

466 pp.; 1993

3. *The Music of Chance*   Paul Auster
Parable about two men, a fireman and a gambler, who end up
in a deadly game against two guys named Flower and Stone.
They risk everything "on the single blind turn of a card."

217 pp.; 1990

4. *Chimera*   John Barth
A modern Scheherazade and *Thousand and One Nights* story.
Barth's Chimera, like the mythical fire-breathing monster, is
composed of three interrelated elements: fore, Dunyazadiad;
hind, Bellerophoniad; and middle, Perseid.   **308 pp.; 1972**

5. *Snow White*   Donald Barthelme
A surrealistic version of the classic fairy tale combined with a

critique of consumer society that also consumes fiction. Also
Sixty Stories.   180 pp.; 1967

6. *Waiting for the End of the World*   Madison Smartt Bell
The ultimate perverse fairy tale—New York as the modern
hell. In *Save Me, Joe Louis*, two drifters, Charlie and Macrae,
who meet in New York's Battery Park, end up killing cops in
Baltimore.   322 pp.; 1985

7. *Mr. Palomar*   Italo Calvino
Mr. Palomar, a descendant of the Baron who lived in the
trees, is a quester after knowledge. A witty, fantastic tale.
                                                    126 pp.; 1983

8. *Nights at the Circus*   Angela Carter
Considered by many critics to be her masterpiece, this tale is
about the adventures of the half girl, half bird named Fevvers.
                                                    294 pp.; 1985

9. *The Alchemist*   Paulo Coelho
Santiago, an Andalusian boy, travels in search of treasure, but
most important is his encounter with the alchemist. Over a
million and a half copies of this modern fable, written by a
Brazilian, have been sold.   177 pp.; 1993

10. *Pinocchio in Venice*   Robert Coover
A postmodern tour de force that is a wicked companion volume to the original Pinocchio story. Older scholar and aes-
thete returns to Italy to complete his magnum opus, a final
great tribute to the Blue-Haired Fairy.   330 pp.; 1991

11. *The Name of the Rose*   Umberto Eco
Signs, symbols, and metaphysical speculation; if you like
medieval thrillers and complicated puzzles, this can't be beat!
                                                    724 pp.; 1983

12. *October Light*   John Gardner
Picture of a family revolution, this allegorical novel is shot
through with legend, memory, and myth. An old brother and
sister live together, but not happily, in his house in Vermont.

Even Ethan Allen becomes a character here, as do the people in a trashy paperback in the sister's room. One of Gardner's last novels; he died young in a motorcycle accident. His novel *Grendel* fits here too.   434 pp.; 1976

13. *The Old Man and the Sea*   Ernest Hemingway
Won the Pulitzer Prize and led directly to his being awarded the Nobel in 1954. In this parablelike tale, an old Cuban fisherman who catches a giant marlin is unable to keep the sharks from mutilating it before he gets to shore. Watch the symbolic number forty in this one.   140 pp.; 1952

14. *Smilla's Sense of Snow*   Peter Hoeg
Smilla, an elegant, independent thirty-seven-year-old woman who is an expert on snow and ice, investigates the death of an Eskimo boy from Greenland named Isaiah who lived in her apartment building in Copenhagen and appears to have fallen from a roof. This morality tale is heightened by the discussion of culture, race, heritage, and destiny, all encoded in the character of Smilla's Eskimo mother and her father, a rational, unemotional Danish anesthesiologist.   453 pp.; 1993

15. *The Bone People*   Keri Hulme
Winner of the Booker Prize and the Pegasus Prize for literature, this unusual novel features Kerewin Holmes, a part Pakeha (New Zealander of European descent), part Maori (New Zealander of Polynesian descent) in self-exile, living in a tower she has built with money won in a lottery. Hulme, herself a Maori, lives in Okarito, Westland, in New Zealand.
                                             450 pp.; 1985

16 *Mrs. Caliban and Other Stories*   Rachel Ingalls
In most fairy tales, there are disappearing children, murder, perversion, and the rest; Ingalls treats all the horrors in a matter-of-fact, clear manner. These are modern fables.
                                             125 pp.; 1983

17. *Einstein's Dreams*   Alan Lightman
Lightman is a science writer (*A Modern Day Yankee in a Connecticut Court*), but in this unusual fiction debut he cre-

ates Einstein's possible nighttime fantasies as a twenty-six-year-old patent clerk in Switzerland, during May and June of 1905, when Einstein was working on his theory of relativity.

224 pp.; 1993

18. *The Giver* Lois Lowry
A haunting novel in which a boy inhabits a seemingly ideal world but where there are dark secrets underlying this fragile perfection. Any reading group could (and should) talk about this slim volume for hours.

180 pp.; 1993

19. *A River Runs Through It* Norman Maclean
Two brothers growing up in Missoula, Montana, in the 1930s learn the art of fly-fishing from their father; when one brother's life becomes fragmented and troubled, the other brother tries to save him. And it is, as usual, much better than the movie.

161 pp.; 1989

20. *The Magic Mountain* Thomas Mann
In this long, celebrated novel devoid of plot, Hans Castorp, a young north German engineer, visits his cousin in a TB sanitorium high in the Swiss mountains. Fascinated by decay, he stays for seven years. Mann uses this framework to discuss all the symbolic and philosophical problems of the twentieth century in what is definitely one of the greatest works of modern world literature.

900 pp.; 1924

21. *Moby-Dick* Herman Melville
Remember how your high school English teacher told you the whiteness of the whale represented good and Ahab symbolized evil? Or was it the other way around? Take another look.

728 pp.; 1851

22. *The Satanic Verses* Salman Rushdie
This fable about Islam earned Rushdie a death sentence from Iranian fundamentalists. He followed their threat with *Haroun and the Sea of Stories. Midnight's Children* is especially recommended.

546 pp.; 1989

23. *The Catcher in the Rye*   J. D. Salinger
Holden Caulfield has entered the vocabulary as a modern-day
Huck Finn and, with his sister, Phoebe, represents (among
many other interpretations) the innocence of Eden and its
corruption by society. The paperback version published in
1964 has gone through more than forty printings. Follow up
with *Franny and Zooey*, the bible of the 1960s.

277 pp.; 1951

24. *Mr. Summer's Story*   Patrick Süskind
The narrator is a nameless boy who hates his piano teacher.
Mr. Summer is an eccentric recluse who strides around the
countryside saying only, "Why can't you just leave me in
peace!" and who pulls the boy down to earth, literally and
emotionally. The drawings by Jean-Jacques Sempé are deli-
cate and pure. Süskind's first novel, a bestseller called *Per-
fume*, was a much harsher book about evil.   116 pp.; 1993

25. *Tintin in the New World*   Frederic Tuten
Tintin, a French comic strip hero beloved by both adults and
children in the glossy, oversized, imported comic book version, is introduced by an American writer into a novel and to
the temptations of the real world.   239 pp.; 1993

26. *Things Invisible to See*   Nancy Willard
One of the few novels that can be described, in the best sense,
as a cult novel among writers. On the surface it is about a
baseball game between dead sports heroes and the mothers of
children who can be saved only if those mothers win the
game. It is actually a brilliant fictionalized discussion of good
and evil.   263 pp.; 1985

27. *Sexing the Cherry*   Jeanette Winterson
Rabelaisian romp in the reign of Charles II when Jordan and
his mother, the Dog-Woman, live on the banks of the stinking
Thames. He learns that every journey conceals another within it.   167 pp.; 1990

28. *Orlando*   Virginia Woolf

A historical fantasy, this novel charts the life of its central character from a masculine identity within the Elizabethan court to a feminine identity. An early exploration of the tension between androgyny and the conventions of sexual difference.   222 pp.; 1928

4

THE BUTLER DID IT? UNLIKELY

Mysteries by Women

1. *Snapshot*   Linda Barnes
Boston P.I. Carlotta Carlyle, a six-foot-one-inch-tall redhead, receives a snapshot of a newborn baby in the mail, and in the next several weeks more photographs of the same child arrive. Barnes's fifth work is about obsession, hypocrisy, and corruption. *Steel Guitar* and *The Snake Tattoo* are good too.
                                            325 pp.; 1993

2. *Death on the Nile*   Agatha Christie
When Christie died in 1976 at the age of eighty-five, she had written sixty-six mystery novels, thirteen short story collections, a book of poems, a volume of Christmas verse and stories, and her autobiography. In this mystery, the inestimable Hercule Poirot is relaxing on a luxury liner when the sound of a shot disturbs the peace. Her female sleuth, Miss Jane Marple, appeared first in *Sleeping Murder* and finally in *The Murder at the Vicarage*. *The Murder of Roger Ackroyd* traces Hercule Poirot on his most baffling case.   **340 pp.; 1938**

3. *I'll Be Seeing You*   Mary Higgins Clark
Clark writes traditional mysteries, this one about a mugging and a Jane Doe victim who looks just like the newspaper reporter investigating the case. Also *Weep No More, My Lady*.   **317 pp.; 1993**

4. *Bloodlines*   **Susan Conant**

A mystery about the disreputable characters who sometimes supply pet shops. Diane Sweet, owner of Puppy Luv, is visited by Conant's hero, dog writer Holly Winter. Hours later Diane is dead and the rescue malamute, Missy, has disappeared. Like her other lighthearted mysteries, *Gone to the Dogs, A New Leash on Death, Dead and Doggone, Bite of Death*, and *Paws Before Dying* are for animal lovers of all kinds.

271 pp.; 1992

5. *All That Remains*   **Patricia D. Cornwell**

Five young couples suffer strange deaths in Virginia. Cornwell's cool detective, Dr. Kay Scarpetta, chief medical examiner (and a forensic pathologist) for the state, investigates. This book was followed by *Cruel and Unusual*. Her first novel, *Postmortem*, won the Edgar (mystery's highest award), Creasey, Anthony, and Macavity awards in the same year.

373 pp.; 1992

6. *Eulogy for a Brown Angel*   **Lucha Corpi**

Corpi, a poet, gives her sleuth occasional clairvoyant moments that provide hints of subtle menace. Good ear for Latino rhythms.   189 pp.; 1992

7. *Death in a Tenured Position*   **Amanda Cross**

As in all the Cross mysteries, the literary detective, Kate Fansler, redoubtable academic and amateur sleuth, solves the case. Read *A Trap for Fools* too. In her "other" life Cross is Carolyn Heilbrun, a literary scholar.   285 pp.; 1981

8. *Well-Schooled Murder*   **Elizabeth George**

This is George's third novel featuring Detective Inspector Thomas Lynley of New Scotland Yard. In this one a boy is missing from a private school and is found murdered—something evil is going on where the elite are educated. *Missing Joseph* has a tiny British village and a murdered vicar but does not resemble Agatha Christie in any way. Also *For the Sake of Elena*.   356 pp.; 1990

9. *"G" is for Gumshoe*   Sue Grafton
"A" is for Alibi, "D" is for Deadbeat, "F" is for Fugitive—
you get the idea—all starring Kinsey Millhone, a tough cookie
in Santa Teresa, California, who is also resourceful and sensitive. She keeps her .32 handgun wrapped in an old sock.

261 pp.; 1990

10. *Love nor Money*   Linda Grant
Catherine Sayler is Grant's sleuth. Here she unravels a murder
and a network of child sexual abuse. Also *Blind Trust*, about
computer scams.   **277 pp.; 1991**

11. *The Horse You Came In On*   Martha Grimes
Superintendent Richard Jury of Scotland Yard and his aristocratic sidekick Melrose Plant are in Baltimore, dealing with
the unrelated(?) murders of an Edgar Allan Poe scholar, a
museum curator, and a derelict. *The Old Contemptibles* is
fine too.   **332 pp.; 1993**

12. *Strangled Prose*   Joan Hess
The widow Claire Malloy supports herself and her teenage
daughter by running a small bookstore in a college town.
When she reluctantly hosts a book-signing party, the author is
strangled shortly afterward. Also *Malice in Maggody* and *A
Really Cute Corpse*.   **183 pp.; 1986**

13. *The Talented Mr. Ripley*   Patricia Highsmith
Ripley is a creepy, endearing antihero; Highsmith is a poetic
writer of mysteries.   **295 pp.; 1992**

14. *A Taste for Death*   P. D. James
Adam Dalgliesh, James's best sleuth, is back in this one just in
time to investigate the deaths of Sir Paul Berowne, rich and
cultivated, and of an alcoholic tramp, both found dead in the
vestry of a London church. Her other famous detective is
Cordelia Grey, particularly good in *An Unsuitable Job for a
Woman*. Read *Devices and Desires* and the newest, *Children
of Men*.   **459 pp.; 1986**

15. *Grievous Sin*   Faye Kellerman
Which parent hasn't worried about this: who would steal a
newborn baby from her mother? Blackmail, a dumb nurse,
and a weight lifter appear in this chilling tale. Read *Days of
Atonement* too.   368 pp.; 1993

16. *Murder at the Gardner*   Jane Langton
Traditional American mystery writer, charming and witty.
Her Homer Kelly mysteries are set in Nantucket, one of
America's most beautiful places, and around Boston. Also
read *The Dante Game*.   353 pp.; 1988

17. *The Hangman's Beautiful*   Sharyn McCrumb
Daughter
McCrumb won the Edgar Award for *Bimbos of the Death
Sun;* the sequel was *Zombies of the Gene Pool*, about murder
at a science fiction convention. This one is set in Appalachia,
where horrible murders take place at the Underhill farm. She
also writes the Elizabeth MacPherson mysteries.

                                                       306 pp.; 1992

18. *Wolf in the Shadows*   Marcia Muller
Sharon McCone, Muller's investigator, takes an unauthorized
leave of absence from All Souls, the do-good legal collective
in San Francisco where she has worked since 1977, and is
involved instead with illegal immigrants in San Diego's underground community. *Trophies and Dead Things* is good too.
Considered by Grafton to be the "founding mother" of contemporary female private-eye mysteries.   384 pp.; 1993

19. *Blanche on the Lam*   Barbara Neely
The detective here, Blanche White (notice the name), is a
middle-aged, working-class African-American. Walter Mosley,
(see no. 21 on the next list), watch out!   180 pp.; 1992

20. *Guardian Angel*   Sara Paretsky
V. I. (Victoria Iphigenia) Warshawski, Paretsky's detective,
daughter of a Jewish-Italian mother, runs into her smug ex-
husband at a charity concert; her neighbor Hattie Frazell slips

in the tub; and V. I. finds herself in the middle of the biggest political scandal to hit Chicago in years. Peretsky has a fan named Bill Clinton. *Indemnity Only, Deadlock*, and others.

469 pp.; 1992

21. *The Face of a Stranger* Anne Perry

Perry's province is the Victorian era. In this novel William Monk, a London police detective who has forgotten everything because of an accident, must deal with the brutal murder of Major the Honorable Joscelin Grey, Crimean war hero and popular man-about-town. Perry lives in the Scottish Highlands. Also *Belgrave Square*. 328 pp.; 1990

22. *The Holy Thief* Ellis Peters

Brother Cadfael, the extraordinary twelfth-century herbalist-detective of the medieval Abbey of St. Peter and St. Paul, returns in a tale of unholy murder. *The Heaven Tree Trilogy* contains *The Heaven Tree, The Green Branch*, and *The Scarlet Seed* (listed under Edith Pargeter). 246 pp.; 1992

23. *A Dark-Adapted Eye* Ruth Rendell

An Edgar Award winner, this is a psychological mystery of childhood and family. This Brit is on everybody's best mystery writer list. Read *The Bridesmaid* too. 264 pp.; 1986

24. *Gaudy Night* Dorothy Sayers

A classic mystery without a murder, this is a love story with a satisfying ending. Her mysteries of the 1920s include *Lord Peter Wimsey*. 469 pp.; 1936

25. *She Walks in Beauty* Sarah Shankman

Samantha Adams, amateur detective and reporter from Atlanta, has just turned forty and is in no mood to cover the Miss America Pageant. She suspects foul play and a treacherous runway, and she's right about both. Sam appears also in *First Kill All the Lawyers, Then Hang All the Liars*, and *Now Let's Talk of Graves*. 289 pp.; 1991

26. *The Axman's Jazz* Julie Smith

Based on a real-life serial killer in 1919 New Orleans. This time around Skip Langdon, Smith's detective, gets involved with a multitude of self-help groups and twelve-step programs. *New Orleans Mourning* won the Edgar, and is enthusiastically recommended. In *Jazz Funeral* the producer of the New Orleans Jazz and Heritage Festival is stabbed to death in his kitchen.   341 pp.; 1991

27. *The Franchise Affair*   Josephine Tey
This novel is based on the real disappearance of a young girl and on the difference between what we assume is guilt and who we assume is innocent. *The Daughter of Time* is the all-time favorite book of many readers.   272 pp.; 1948

28. *The Lies That Bind*   Judith Van Gieson
Van Gieson's protagonist is Neil Hamel, a tough, funny Albuquerque lawyer. Here she gets mixed up with, among other things, real estate boondoggles, Santa Fe's polo set, psychic entrepreneurs, and the homeless.   256 pp.; 1993

29. *Anna's Book*   Barbara Vine (Ruth Rendell)
By an Edgar-winning author, this wonderful novel concerns the diary entries of Anna, a turn-of-the-century Danish immigrant and her granddaughter. Don't miss *A Fatal Inversion* and *King Solomon's Carpet*.   394 pp.; 1993

Mysteries by Men

1. *Out on the Cutting Edge*   Lawrence Block
Matt Scudder, a defrocked New York cop, is the hard-drinking hero here, although in this one he's off booze. Block's books are as much about New York, beyond the Sixth Precinct and Midtown North, as they are about crime. *Eight Million Ways to Die* and *Some Days You Get the Bear* are also recommended.   260 pp.; 1989

2. *Black Cherry Blues*   James Lee Burke
Third in a series featuring ex–New Orleans cop Dave Robicheaux, Vietnam vet, widower whose wife was murdered in their bed, recovering alcoholic, father to an adopted Sal-

vadoran child, and son of an illiterate Cajun who was killed on an oil rig. *A Stained White Radiance* and all of the Robicheaux novels are recommended.   290 pp.; 1989

3. *The Big Sleep*   Raymond Chandler

This is the first of Chandler's novels with Detective Philip Marlowe as the hero. The others are *Farewell, My Lovely, The High Window*, and *The Lady in the Lake*.

                                                    155 pp.; 1939

4. *The Woman Who Walked Into the Sea*   Philip R. Craig

If you can't get to Martha's Vineyard, read the Jeff Jackson mysteries for the details, correct down to the smoked bluefish pâté. Jackson, a former Boston cop and now a Vineyard fisherman, turns up in *Cliff Hanger* too.   215 pp.; 1991

5. *The Mexican Tree Duck*   James Crumley

In his first novel in ten years Crumley returns with P.I. C. W. Sughrue, last seen in *The Last Good Kiss*. Here he tries to find a beautiful kidnapped woman.   256 pp.; 1993

6. *The Riddle of the Third Mile*   Colin Dexter

In this mystery British Detective Chief Inspector Morse of the Thames Valley Police must deal with a mutilated corpse found floating in the Oxford Canal and the disappearance of Oliver Maximilian Alexander Browne-Smith, a cantankerous Oxford professor. *The Way Through the Woods* is a new one by Dexter.   224 pp.; 1983

7. *Longshot*   Dick Francis

A writer waiting for his novel to hit the bestseller list starts a biography of a racehorse trainer, which means danger in rural England. Also *Blood Sport*, about stolen stallions.

                                                    320 pp.; 1990

8. *The Glass Key*   Dashiell Hammett

The film *Miller's Crossing* used this plot. A gangster named Ned Beaumont turns into a detective in order to save his own life. *Red Harvest* is as much a western as a mystery. Hammett invented Sam Spade.   **285 pp.; 1931**

9. *Strip Tease*   **Carl Hiaasen**
As Congressman David Dilbeck says, "I should never be around naked women." This time, between the strippers and the sugar growers in Florida, he gets into plenty of trouble. Hiaasen, a newspaper reporter in Miami, can really write. Also *Skin Tight, Native Tongue*.   **354 pp.; 1993**

10. *Coyote Waits*   **Tony Hillerman**
The murder of a Navajo tribal policeman and an ancient artifact are connected. *Skinwalkers* followed. (In Navajo legend, a skinwalker is a Navajo who does not follow the path of beauty.)   **292 pp.; 1990**

11. *Private Eyes*   **Jonathan Kellerman**
The detective here, Alex Delaware, is also a psychologist. He comes to the rescue of an actress menaced by someone recently released from prison. *Time Bomb* is good too. *Blood Test* is a serial-killer story and ultraviolent. *When the Bough Breaks* deals with child molestation.   **475 pp.; 1992**

12. *The Day the Rabbi Resigned*   **Harry Kemelman**
Rabbi David Small, the most unorthodox rebbe in or out of *schul*, has been around for twenty-five years. Now he wants out of Barnard's Crossing but ends up searching for the killer of Victor Joyce, local and unloved college professor. The rabbi appears in nine Kemelman mysteries, *Monday the Rabbi Took Off, Tuesday the Rabbi Saw Red, Wednesday the Rabbi Got Wet*, etc.   **273 pp.; 1992**

13. *The Spy Who Came In from the Cold*   **John le Carré**
This was a runaway bestseller thirty years ago, and it still works. The spy wants to quit the business, but somehow he can't get out.   **256 pp.; 1964**

14. *Maximum Bob*   **Elmore Leonard**
His twenty-ninth novel, and this time the crackpot judge (see title) in Palm Beach County, Florida, tries to get rid of his

wife by introducing an alligator into their happy home. *Rum Punch* is good too, and *Pronto*, the newest, is great.

304 pp.; 1991

15. *The Road to Omaha*   **Robert Ludlum**
In this funny thriller a master of suspense resurrects his two most outrageous characters, General MacKensie Lochinvar Hawkins—the Hawk—and Harvard-educated legal wizard Sam Devereaux. Our Yale-educated president reads Ludlum. Also *The Road to Gandolpho, The Scorpio Illusion.*

487 pp.; 1992

16. *Eight Black Horses*   **Ed McBain**
McBain (who is the author Evan Hunter) writes the "Eighty-seventh Precinct Mysteries," and in this one a very naked dead woman is somehow connected to the odd messages being received at the station house. (Remember the Dead Man from previous McBain novels? He's back!) Also *Mischief.*

250 pp.; 1985

17. *The Song Dog*   **James McClure**
In this prequel, harking back to 1962, we learn how McClure's ratchet-tongued South African detective, Lieutenant Tromp Kramer, met his Zulu partner, Sergeant Mickey Zondi. *The Artful Egg* is great too. *Mary, Mary* features the Florida criminal attorney Matthew Hope.   **274 pp.; 1991**

18. *The Blue Hammer*   **Ross Macdonald**
One of the best Lew Archer mysteries. Macdonald, Richard Hugo, Charles Willeford, James Crumley, and James Lee Burke are all considered third-wave naturalistic writers; they are famous for gritty realism and strong characters.

270 pp.; 1976

19. *Strange Loyalties*   **William McIlvanney**
Glasgow Detective Jack Laidlaw tries to find sense in the death of his brother, a talented painter, and to understand why this "accident" happened. Philosophical and dark. Read *Laidlaw* and *The Papers of Tony Veitch* too.   **281 pp.; 1992**

20. *Rumpole à la Carte*   John Mortimer
Eighth collection of stories about this rumpled barrister who
became famous on the PBS television show.   246 pp.; 1990

21. *Devil in a Blue Dress*   Walter Mosley
Easy Rawlins, Mosley's detective, is an African-American
who fights crime and prejudice in the 1950s. And President
Clinton is one of his biggest fans. Read *White Butterfly* too.
                                                    215 pp.; 1990

22. *Pastime*   Robert B. Parker
In the eighteenth of Parker's Spenser novels, we get a sense of
this Boston detective's childhood and his initiation into man-
hood. *Promised Land* and *Paper Doll*, set in the South, are
recommended as well.   342 pp.; 1991

23. *A First Class Murder*   Elliot Roosevelt
Ninth in a series by the now-dead author, and featuring his
mother, Eleanor. In this one it's 1938, and the *Normandie* is
sailing from France to New York; the Dr. Watson figure turns
out to be John F. Kennedy.   261 pp.; 1991

24. *McNally's Secret*   Lawrence Sanders
The sleuth Archy Sanders gets stuck to priceless stamps. *The
Anderson Tapes* is good too.   317 pp.; 1992

25. *Maigret in Holland*   Georges Simenon
French Inspector Maigret arrives in Delfzijl to find out who
murdered Conrad Popinga, a teacher. Watch that Manila
cigar butt on the dining room carpet.   165 pp.; 1993

26. *Gorky Park*   Martin Cruz Smith
Three bodies found frozen together in a Moscow park are
only the beginning in this landmark thriller. Smith followed
with *Red Square;* Investigator Arkady Renko returns from
exile on the Polar Star fleet. Also read *Polar Star*.
                                                    365 pp.; 1981

27. *The League of Frightened Men*   Rex Stout
Mysteries and Nero Wolfe are synonymous. The detective
weighs one-seventh of a ton, has a collection of 10,000

orchids, and obviously loves food. Read *The Black Echo* too.

217 pp.; 1982

28. *Pop. 1280*   **Jim Thompson**
Thompson is a hard-boiled crime writer, but his small-town sheriff, Nick Corey, gets the job done here. *The Grifters* became the movie with Anjelica Huston. *The Killer Inside Me* is a portrait of a psychopathic killer.   **217 pp.; 1990**

29. *Brothers Keeper*   **Donald Westlake**
Great title for a comic thriller about Brother Benedict and his fight to save the Manhattan Crispite Monastery from someone who seems familiar . . . if you've heard of Donald Trump. Westlake writes the Dormunder novels; *Don't Ask* is a tale of two new east European countries fighting over the remains of a 600-year-old saint.   **254 pp.; 1975**

5

NATIVE AMERICAN LITERATURE

1. *The Lone Ranger and Tonto* **Sherman Alexie**
  Fistfight in Heaven
Twenty-two widely praised short stories by a young member
of the Spokane Nation, often about the alcoholism, malnutri-
tion, and suicidal self-loathing that plague *some* Native
Americans. His debut collection was *The Business of Fancy
Dancing*. **223 pp.; 1993**

2. *The Sacred Hoop* **Paula Gunn Allen**
Allen, a Laguna Pueblo poet, novelist, and scholar, argues
that colonization transformed and obscured what were once
woman-centered cultures. She explores a range of female
deities, American Indian women's history, the place of lesbians in Indian culture, and the importance of mothers and
grandmothers to Indian identity. **285 pp.; 1986**

3. *Night Flying Woman* **Ignatia Broker**
This is an Ojibway narrative of life in the nineteenth century
and the story of the author's great-great-grandmother, Ni-bo-
Wi-se-gwe, or Night Flying Woman **135 pp.; 1983**

4. *Turtle Meat: And Other Stories* **Joseph Bruchac**
A collection of seventeen original stories that span time from

the mythic past to the present, by the author of *Thirteen Moons on Turtle's Back* (also recommended).   **144 pp.; 1992**

5. *From the River's Edge*   Elizabeth Cook-Lynn
John Tatekeya, a cattleman, discovers what it means to be a Dakotah in the white man's court when the Missouri River Power Project floods reservation lands and forty-two of his prized horned Herefords are stolen.   **147 pp.; 1991**

6. *Custer Died for Your Sins*   Vine Deloria, Jr.
Published when the American Indian Movement (AIM) was just a year old, this book was the clarion call of a new militancy among Native Americans. It has been updated with a new preface.   **279 pp.; 1969**

7. *A Yellow Raft in Blue Water*   Michael Dorris
This is a thrice-told tale of three women: Rayona, a fifteen-year-old who is part black; her American Indian mother, Christine; and the fierce and mysterious Ida, a mother and grandmother whose secrets and dreams braid the three lives together.   **372 pp.; 1987**

8. *Tracks*   Louise Erdrich
The prequel to *Love Medicine* and *The Beet Queen, Tracks* is told in two different voices—that of Nanapush, a wise leader of the Chippewa; and Pauline, torn between her Chippewa and Christian beliefs. At the center is Fleur Pillager, the witch-like avenger.   **226 pp.; 1988**

9. *Firesticks*   Diane Glancy
Surrealistic, experimental stories (or firesticks) by a Cherokee poet. Recurring themes are transformation through flight and the stitching together of cultures.   **142 pp.; 1993**

10. *The Jailing of Cecilia Capture*   Janet Campbell Hale
Engrossing story by a member of the Coeur d'Alene tribe of northern Idaho that takes off when Cecilia Eagle Capture, a married mother of two and a law student at Berkeley, is arrested for drunk driving on her thirtieth birthday, Hale's new book, *Bloodlines: Odyssey of a Native Daughter*, is a

collection of autobiographical essays, largely about growing up in a troubled family. Highly recommended.

201 pp.; 1985

11. *In Mad Love and War*   Joy Harjo
Winner of the Poetry Society of America's William Carlos Williams Award for 1990, this short book of poems is written by a member of the Creek tribe who teaches at a western university. An exceptional collection.   **65 pp.; 1990**

12. *Rising Voices*   selected by Arlene B. Hirschfelder
and Beverly B. Singer
Writings of young people, including sixty-two poems and essays, that mirror the richness and sorrow of the Native American experience. *Happily May I Walk* (by Hirschfelder) is also highly recommended.   **115 pp.; 1992**

13. *Mean Spirit*   Linda Hogan
Extraordinary fictionalized account of what happened when oil was discovered on land in Oklahoma, in the 1920s and 1930s, and Osage Indians began to die. Rampant fraud, intimidation, and murder—perpetrated by white people—are revealed.   **377 pp.; 1990**

14. *Green Grass, Running Water*   Thomas King
First-rate comic novel about Lionel Red Dog, a Canadian Blackfoot stereo and TV salesman, his Uncle Eli Stands Alone, and his sister Latisha (who runs the Dead Dog Cafe). Read *Medicine River* too.   **360 pp.; 1993**

15. *Wind from an Enemy Sky*   D'Arcy McNickle
The dean of American Indian writers, McNickle, a Flathead, writes of the tragedy caused by the building of a dam and by the stubbornness of misunderstanding in two opposing worlds.   **256 pp.; 1978**

16. *In the Spirit of Crazy Horse*   Peter Matthiessen
To quote Dee Brown, this is "the first solidly documented account of the U.S. government's renewed assault upon American Indians that began in the 1970s."   **628 pp.; 1983**

17. *House Made of Dawn*   **N. Scott Momaday**
Pulitzer Prize–winning novel of a proud stranger in his native
land.   **192 pp.; 1968**

18. *Woven Stone*   **Simon Ortiz**
An omnibus consisting of three previous books—*Going for
the Rain, A Good Journey*, and *Fight Back: For the Sake of
the People, For the Sake of the Land*—by an Acoma Pueblo
who is one of America's best poets.   **350 pp.; 1992**

19. *Wolfsong*   **Louis Owens**
Tom Joseph, a young Indian who is away at college, returns
for his uncle's funeral and finds himself caught up in the old
man's fight to save the wilderness from destruction.
                                                  256 pp.; 1991

20. *Ceremony*   **Leslie Marmon Silko**
Tayo, a young American Indian who was a Japanese prisoner
of war during World War II, returns to the Laguna Pueblo
reservation to search for resolution. That quest leads to the
ancient stories of his people. Silko's *Almanac of the Dead* is a
controversial, end-of-the-world-is-coming novel.
                                                  262 pp.; 1977

21. *A Lakota Woman's Story*   **Madonna Swan**
Mark St. Pierre, a professor at Colorado Mountain College,
records here multiple versions of the Lakota legends told to
him by Swan, as well as stories of the ten years she spent in
sanitoriums fighting her tuberculosis. There is some confusion about how much is Swan and what St. Pierre con-
tributed.   **209 pp.; 1990**

22. *Talking Indian*   **Anna Lee Walters**
Walters, a Pawnee/Otoe living on the Navajo reservation in
Arizona, collects her autobiography, short stories, historical
tribal documentation, and more. Very fine.   **222 pp.; 1992**

23. *Winter in the Blood*   **James Welch**
The thirty-two-year-old narrator, a sensitive and intelligent
Blackfeet Indian, symbolizes the dispossession of his people

and the nation's indifference to their fate. In *The In* *Lawyer* Sylvester Yellow Calf, a graduate of Stanford Lav. is a long way from the Blackfeet reservation in Browning, Montana.   **176 pp.; 1974**

24. *Pieces of White Shell:*   **Terry Tempest Williams**
    A Journey to Navajoland
This first book won the 1984 Southwest Book Award and is a memoir of time spent teaching on a Navajo reservation. Williams also wrote *Coyote's Canyon*.   **162 pp.; 1984**

25. *Black Eagle Child*   **Ray A. Young Bear**
Intricate stories about religion, myth, dreams, poverty, and injustice by a Mesquakie writer who re-creates his life in Iowa in the 1950s through the 1970s.   **261 pp.; 1992**

6

GO WEST

1. *Strange Angels*   **Jonis Agee**
Set in the Nebraska sandhills, this is a world of cowboys, honky-tonk bars, small towns, and huge stretches of rolling prairie. Also the story of Arthur, the legitimate heir of Heywood Bennett, the late patriarch of a Nebraska ranching family, and of his bastard brother, Cody. Agee wrote *Sweet Eyes* and *Bend This Heart*.   **405 pp.; 1993**

2. *All but the Waltz*   **Mary Clearman Blew**
Essays about an ordinary but also remarkable Montana family, about whom we come to care deeply.   **223 pp.; 1991**

3. *Desierto*   **Charles Bowden**
Subtitled *Memories of the Future*. Bowden evokes here the southwestern desert and the men and women who inhabit it: tycoons, drug kingpins, the aboriginal Seris and Yaquis, and the author himself.   **225 pp.; 1991**

4. *The Ox-Bow Incident*   **Walter V. T. Clark**
This novel about a Nevada lynching was followed with *The Track of the Cat*, about brothers hunting for a mountain lion.   **309 pp.; 1940**

5. *A Garlic Testament*   **Stanley Crawford**
Subtitled *Seasons on a Small New Mexico Farm*. The crop is

the subject here, but "place" holds sway too. Crawford's first nonfiction book, *Mayordomo: Chronicle of an Acequia in North New Mexico*, was about his experience overseeing the local irrigation ditch. He is also a novelist.   **241 pp.; 1992**

6. *Deadwood* **Pete Dexter**
Set on the Dakota frontier in the days of Wild Bill Hickok, this second novel is by the author of *God's Pocket* and *Brotherly Love*, two Philadelphia stories.   **365 pp.; 1986**

7. *This House of Sky* **Ivan Doig**
Award-winning novel followed by *Dancing at the Rascal Fair*, set in the great Montana highlands.   **314 pp.; 1978**

8. *The River Why* **David James Duncan**
This is the story of Gus Orviston, fly-fishing genius, and of his adventures with a woman, a river, many trout, several dogs, a philosopher, a salmon, and a colorful cast of backwoods characters.   **294 pp.; 1983**

9. *Drinking Dry Clouds* **Gretel Ehrlich**
Eloquent linked stories of whites and Japanese Americans interned at Wyoming's Heart Mountain during World War II. Since Ehrlich lives on a ranch in northern Wyoming, it's not surprising that she wrote *The Solace of Open Spaces*, also highly recommended.   **160 pp.; 1991**

10. *Wildlife* **Richard Ford**
Fourth novel, written in spare, moving prose and set in Great Falls, Montana. *Wildlife* chronicles how a family's sense of itself is changed by surrounding and rampant forest fires. *Rock Springs*, a collection of short stories, was highly praised.   **177 pp.; 1990**

11. *The Meadow* **James Galvin**
An unusual, touching, one-hundred-year history of a meadow in the arid mountains of the Colorado-Wyoming border.   **230 pp.; 1992**

12. *The Jump-Off Creek* **Molly Gloss**
Winner of the 1990 Pacific Northwest Booksellers Associa-

tion Award for Fiction, this is a portrait of a pioneer woman, Lydia Sanderson, and her struggles as she homesteads alone in the Blue Mountains of Oregon in the 1890s. **186 pp.; 1989**

13. *The Big Sky*   **A. B. Guthrie**
Guthrie moved a quarter century into the past to portray the West, from Kentucky to Oregon. He wrote the screenplay for the movie *Shane*. **386 pp.; 1947**

14. *Desperadoes*   **Ron Hansen**
Geoffrey Wolff called this novel "one of the great prose entertainments of recent years." It is generally considered to be one of the great contemporary novels of the West. Also *The Assassination of Jesse James by the Coward Robert Ford*.
273 pp.; 1979

15. *Seven Rivers West*   **Edward Hoagland**
Hoagland lives in the East, but he re-creates the Native American West of the 1880s in the fictional town of Horse Swim. His essay collections include *The Courage of Turtles*, *Walking the Dead*, *Diamond River*, and *The Tugman's Passage*.
319 pp.; 1986

16. *Cowboys Are My Weakness*   **Pam Houston**
Terrific short stories, mostly in the first person, told by women who get mixed up with complicated men, sometimes on a raft in white water. Houston has perfect pitch; she's one to watch. **171 pp.; 1992**

17. *Riding the White Horse Home*   **Teresa Jordan**
Ranch life and social customs in Wyoming, written in beautiful prose. **219 pp.; 1993**

18. *Sometimes a Great Notion*   **Ken Kesey**
This novel about a family and a lumbering feud in Oregon is a more impressive and important book than his hugely popular *One Flew Over the Cuckoo's Nest*. **628 pp.; 1964**

19. *Hole in the Sky*   **William Kittredge**
Here is a searing indictment of Kittredge's own self-destruc-

tive life and of the ways his family's agribusiness empire laid waste to an edemic swatch of Oregon countryside.

238 pp.; 1992

20. *All New People*   **Anne Lamott**
A beautifully honest book about Lamott's life as a single mother in California, her son, Sam, and the support of her church and AA groups.   **166 pp.; 1989**

21. *The Legacy of Conquest*   **Patricia Limerick**
Subtitled *The Unbroken Past of the American West*. Limerick is a popular and respected favorite of westerners. **396 pp.;1987**

22. *Rain or Shine*   **Cyra McFadden**
McFadden writes about her wildly dysfunctional family, particularly her father, a radio announcer on the macho rodeo circuit.   **177 pp.; 1986**

23. *The Bushwacked Piano*   **Thomas McGuane**
Here the popular McGuane satirizes cowboys and conmen from Michigan to Montana. Also *Ninety-two in the Shade*.

220 pp.; 1971

24. *Young Men and Fire*   **Norman Maclean**
This winner of the 1992 National Book Critics Circle Award is an account of the 1949 Mann Gulch fire in Montana that killed thirteen young Forest Service smoke jumpers trapped between the flames and a mountain ridge. More profoundly, it is a book about mortality and the way accidents often control fate.   **301 pp.; 1992**

25. *Streets of Laredo*   **Larry McMurtry**
A Texas bounty hunter goes south of the border as he pursues a train robber and killer. *Lonesome Dove* is McMurtry's best-known book.   **843 pp.; 1993**

26. *The Milagro Beanfield War*   **John Nichols**
After Joe Mondragon taps into the main irrigation channel on a patch of now-arid land, his beanfield in California becomes the rallying point for the small farmers and sheepmen. Down-

state in the capital the Anglo water barons and power brokers have their own multimillion-dollar land development ideas.

445 pp.; 1974

27. *Beyond Deserving* Sandra Scofield
In this second novel, Scofield creates three couples woven together by extended-family ties in a small Oregon town. It won an American Book Award and a New American Fiction Award, as did *Gringa*, her debut book. *Walking Dunes*, her third novel, tells David Puckett's story of life on the wrong side of the tracks in a 1950s Texas town. **310 pp.; 1992**

28. *Making History* Carolyn See
See traces the tragedies of a fragile family living in Los Angeles on the edge of the Pacific rim. Read *Golden Days* too. This writer understands the nuances of California life better than anyone. **276 pp.; 1991**

29. *Angle of Repose* Wallace Stegner
Pulitzer Prize–winning novel about a historian who wants to chronicle his grandparents' story and begins instead to understand his own. The late writer both celebrated the West and criticized the illusions that have been built around it. Also *Where the Bluebird Sings to the Lemonade Springs, The Big Rock Candy Mountain*, and *Sound of Mountain Water*.

569 pp.; 1971

30. *The Best of the West 5* James Thomas and
Denise Thomas
New stories from the "wide side of the Missouri" that explore the western landscape, with all its contradictions and vitality. **256 pp.; 1992**

31. *The Eagle Bird* Charles Wilkinson
As Wallace Stegner said, "Wilkinson understands western attitudes, western inferiorities, western limitations, western pride and arrogance. He is hopeful that the West will arrive at workable compromises before it is destroyed by the big corporations of the extractive industries, or by its more native stockraisers and lumbermen and miners." Amen. **203 pp.; 1992**

7

NEW YORK STORIES

1. *New York Trilogy*   **Paul Auster**
In *City of Glass* Quinn, a mystery writer, receives a phone call
in the middle of the night from someone who is looking for
"Paul Auster. Of the Auster Detective Agency." Thus begins
City of Glass, Volume 1 in this Kafkalike adventure. Volume 2
is *Ghosts*, followed by *The Locked Room*. In my view, Auster
is one of the ten best writers in the United States.

203 pp.; 1985

2. *Mr. Sammler's Planet*   **Saul Bellow**
Artur Sammler, born in Cracow but with the manners of an
Oxford don, looks back on civilized England and the animals
who ran the death camps in World War II. Recommended too
are *The Victim* and *Herzog*.   **316 pp.; 1970**

3. *Breakfast at Tiffany's:*   **Truman Capote**
    A Short Novel and Three Stories
Holly Golightly takes New York, but in most of our minds
she will forever look like Audrey Hepburn.   **179 pp.; 1958**

4. *Happy All the Time*   **Laurie Colwin**
Funny, poignant tale of romance and complications. Colwin
died suddenly at forty-eight; her posthumously published
novel is *A Big Storm Knocked It Over*.   **213 pp.; 1978**

5. *The Old Neighborhood*   Avery Corman
The author of *Kramer vs. Kramer* deals here with what it means to leave a place (in this case, the Bronx), to be someone else, to do something else.   219 pp.; 1980

6. *Sleeping Arrangements*   Laura Cunningham
Entrancing and unusual memoir (which reads like good fiction) of an orphaned Bronx girl, Rosie, raised by two bachelor uncles and their nutty mother, "Esther in Hebrew, Edna in English, and Etka in Russian." Don't miss it.   195 pp.; 1989

7. *Sister Carrie*   Theodore Dreiser
In one of America's finest naturalistic novels, the city is a metaphor for the survival of the fittest: the midwesterner Carrie Meeber survives, and the ill-fated Hurstwood ends up in Potter's Field.   557 pp.; 1900

8. *Life Is Hot in Cracktown*   Buddy Giovinazzo
A debut collection of disturbing tales of life on the edge in New York City's drug-infested neighborhoods—a world of addicts, pimps, prostitutes, transsexuals, homeless people, and criminals. Don't miss "Miss Lonely Has a Date Tonight."   228 pp.; 1993

9. *Useful Gifts*   Carole L. Glickfield
Most of the terrific stories in this debut collection are first-person narratives about Ruthie Zimmer, a little girl who lives with her older siblings and her deaf-mute parents in Manhattan during the 1940s and 1950s.   209 pp.; 1989

10. *Slaves of New York*   Tama Janowitz
Collection of tales about various women in New York—a jewelry designer, an East Village performance artist, and a well-born prostitute, among others, who waft, half-cheerful, half-lost, through the big city. Janowitz wrote *A Cannibal in Manhattan* and *The Male Cross-Dresser Support Group*.   278 pp.; 1986

11. *Gentlemen Prefer Blondes*   **Anita Loos**
This is not on any politically correct list, but if you read between the lines this just might be a feminist text!

217 pp.; 1925

12. *Bright Lights, Big City*   **Jay McInerney**
Considered by many to be the diary of life in the Big Apple during the 1980s, it falls someplace between a beach book and a literary novel. McInerney is a wunderkind of the so-called brat pack of contemporary fiction. Also *Brightness Falls*.   **182 pp.; 1984**

13. *Brown Girl, Brownstones*   **Paule Marshall**
Semiautobiographical novel by a writer who was born in Brooklyn of parents who emigrated from Barbados during World War I. Her latest novel is *Daughters*.   **310 pp.; 1959**

14. *Up in the Old Hotel*   **Joseph Mitchell**
Consists of four of Mitchell's five books—*McSorley's Wonderful Saloon, Old Mr. Flood, The Bottom of the Harbor*, and *Joe Gould's Secret*—along with some pieces never reprinted since their use in the *New Yorker* between 1938 and 1964.   **718 pp.; 1993**

15. *In Nueva York*   **Nicolasa Mohr**
Short, interlocking stories that depict life in one of New York City's Puerto Rican communities.   **194 pp.; 1977**

16. *New York Days*   **Willie Morris**
Morris, the former editor in chief of *Harper's* magazine, recalls the heady literary world in the Big Apple in the 1960s, in the decade of Vietnam and the assassinations.

396 pp.; 1993

17. *Jazz*   **Toni Morrison**
Set in 1920s Harlem, this novel revolves around a triangle: a discontented middle-aged black married couple, Joe and Violet, and the young, seductive woman who changes the equation.   **229 pp.; 1992**

18. *Benediction at the Savoia*   Christine O'Hagan
Irish-Catholic life in the 1960s in Jackson Heights, Queens;
fifteen minutes from Manhattan but insular and unchanging.
For all the impact of glitzy New York City on these people,
they might as well have been in Toledo.   325 pp.; 1992

19. *New York Cookbook*   Molly O'Neill
New York is not New York without dim sum, falafel,
Jamaican meat pies, Hungarian szekely, parantha, and focac-
cia. And a bagel with a schmear wouldn't hurt either. The stories of New York's neighborhood cooks by the *New York
Times* food columnist are great! And your reading club needs
something to eat anyhow.   509 pp.; 1992

20. *Bigfoot Dreams*   Francine Prose
Hilarious story of Vera Perl, star reporter for a sleazoid
tabloid, and what happens when one of her invented stories
turns out to be true! *Women and Children First* is recommended too.   289 pp.; 1986

21. *Call It Sleep*   Henry Roth
Undisputed American masterpiece by an author whose second book was published sixty years later, this is the story of
an immigrant Jewish boy, David Schearl, in the slums of New
York City. Violence in the streets, the terror of poverty, the
sexual conflicts of his parents—no one has dealt with this
kind of material more effectively.   447 pp.; 1934

22. *Rameau's Niece*   Cathleen Schine
A witty send-up of academia plus a love story. The "cultural
elite" should be furious, but the rest of you will love it. Read
To the Birdhouse too.   288 pp.; 1993

23. *Leaving Brooklyn*   Lynne Sharon Schwartz
A novel about double vision; one kind is physical—a wandering eye resulting from a birth injury—and the other is an
emotional insight into the world beyond postwar Brooklyn in
the 1950s.   160 pp.; 1989

24. *Bronx Primitive*   Kate Simon
After Kaila and her family leave the Warsaw ghetto for America at the end of World War I, her neighborhood around 178th Street and Lafontaine Avenue in the Bronx becomes home. Simon recalls an Old Country childhood in the New World, not all of it sweet *or* nurturing.   179 pp.; 1982

25. *A Tree Grows in Brooklyn*   Betty Smith
Unforgettable American masterpiece about a young girl's coming-of-age at the turn of the century.   432 pp.; 1947

26. *Straitjacket and Tie*   Eugene Stein
A phantasmagoric Manhattan where Phillip Rosenbaum has a psychotic breakdown and communicates with extraterrestrials through radio channels no one else can hear. A funny, poignant book.   256 pp.; 1993

27. *New York in the 50's*   Dan Wakefield
Wakefield migrated from Indianapolis to become a novelist and freelance journalist in New York City during the decade of Eisenhower, Jack Kerouac, and the infamous Joe McCarthy.
                                             355 pp.; 1993

28. *Bonfire of the Vanities*   Tom Wolfe
Skip the movie; read the book. You've heard the one about how anything that can go wrong, will? This is a cartoon version of New York, complete with class warfare and seething ethnic resentments, all filtered through the decidedly reactionary view of Wolfe.   659 pp.; 1987

8

SOUTHERN COMFORT

1. *The Revolution of Little Girls*   Blanche McCrary Boyd
Continues with the themes in her essay collection, *The Redneck Way of Knowledge*, and her previous novel, *Mourning the Death of Magic*: disaffected and haunted southerners in the South Carolina low country who can never NOT go home again.   **205 pp.; 1991**

2. *Cold Sassy Tree*   Olive Ann Burns
Will Tweedy is a feisty young schoolteacher who captures the heart of a Georgia town. Burns died in 1990 after working for five years on the sequel, *Leaving Cold Sassy*.
391 pp.; 1984

3. *Prince of Tides*   Pat Conroy
Spanning forty years, it is the story of Tom Wingo, his gifted and troubled twin sister, Savannah, and the dark and violent past of the extraordinary South Carolina family into which they were somewhat unfortunately born. Much better, as usual, than the movie.   **567 pp.; 1986**

4. *Forms of Shelter*   Angela Davis-Gardner
The heart of this beautifully written novel is the betrayal of a girl child—by an absent father, a childish and complicit mother, an evil and devious stepfather, and a confused

brother. Don't miss this one. Davis-Gardner's first novel was *Felice*.   **276 pp.; 1991**

5. *The Floatplane Notebooks*   **Clyde Edgerton**
North Carolinean Albert Copeland keeps a family record in some notebooks he bought to log the flights of his home-built floatplane, a project begun in 1956 when his children were young. Edgerton ranges back one hundred years, to the bride who planted wisteria by her back porch, and returns to the present, when times are different but people are pretty much the same.   **265 pp.; 1988**

6. *Light in August*   **William Faulkner**
A story of sexual passion and racism; Faulkner returns to Yoknapatawpha County to trace the parallel destinies of Lena Grove and Joe Christmas. Not for the fainthearted but wonderful, pure Faulkner.   **313 pp.; 1932**

7. *Fried Green Tomatoes at the*   **Fannie Flagg**
    Whistle Stop Cafe
Hey, more than you think goes on in rural Alabama, including a sexual relationship that was left out of the movie.

                                        403 pp.; 1987

8. *Ellen Foster*   **Kaye Gibbons**
Stark and affecting story of a young country girl in North Carolina whose mother commits suicide and whose father, a tobacco farmer, drinks himself to death. Gibbons is also the author of, among others, *A Cure for Dreams*. **146 pp.; 1987**

9. *The Anna Papers*   **Ellen Gilchrist**
Anna Hand, dying of cancer, returns to Charlotte, North Carolina, to sort out her unresolved conflicts with her sister, old lovers, her brother, and his out-of-wedlock daughter. Gilchrist's *Victory over Japan*, a collection of short stories, won the 1984 American Book Award. **277 pp.; 1988**

10. *Father Melancholy's Daughter*   **Gail Godwin**
A magnificent story of a severely depressed but loving Episcopal cleric, a wife who leaves him for another woman, and his

very intelligent and lonely young daughter, who is the link between them. Godwin lives in upstate New York but is from Asheville, North Carolina. *The Odd Woman* is good too.

404 pp.; 1991

11. *White People*   **Allan Gurganus**
Contains a novella and ten short stories, all by the acclaimed southern writer of *The Oldest Living Confederate Widow Tells All*.   **252 pp.; 1991**

12. *Boomerang*   **Barry Hannah**
Tender weaving of novel and autobiography as the narrator meets Yelverston, a sixty-two-year-old man whose stature and sad nobility astound him.   **150 pp.; 1989**

13. *Dreams of Sleep*   **Josephine Humphreys**
The power of place and the effects of memory reverberate in a house in Charleston, South Carolina, in the debut novel of one of the best writers in the South. *Rich in Love* is also wonderful.   **232 pp.; 1984**

14. *To Kill a Mockingbird*   **Harper Lee**
1961 Pulitzer Prize–winning novel about a small-town lawyer in Alabama who stands up for what is right when a black man is accused of rape. Told from the perspective of his precocious daughter, "Scout."   **296 pp.; 1960**

15. *Tending to Virginia*   **Jill McCorkle**
Three generations of women gather around North Carolinian Ginny Sue to help her at the end of a hard pregnancy. Many clubs read *Crash Diet*.   **312 pp.; 1987**

16. *After the War*   **Richard Marius**
A wounded World War I veteran, Paul Alexander—Greek by birth, Belgian by adoption—is washed up on the shores of Bourbonville, Tennessee, and becomes drawn into the suddenly contentious life of the town.   **622 pp.; 1992**

17. *Shiloh and Other Stories*   **Bobbie Ann Mason**
Stories about working-class people in Kentucky who experience the tension between history and progress as the rural areas where they live become urbanized.   **247 pp.; 1982**

18. *A Good Man Is Hard to Find*   **Flannery O'Connor**
    and Other Stories
O'Connor died young of lupus but left us stories filled with grotesque characters who epitomize false piety and moral blindness. She wrote two novels, *Wise Blood* and *The Violent Bear It Away*.   **251 pp.; 1955**

19. *Love in the Ruins*   **Walker Percy**
This is a great apocalyptic satire and very funny. Percy is the author of *The Moviegoer* and *The Last Gentleman*.
                                    403 pp.; 1971

20. *Fast Lanes*   **Jayne Anne Phillips**
Seven short stories—bold, tough, and pure—from a West Virginian who moved to Massachusetts in order to look back. *Black Tickets* is a fine collection too.   **148 pp.; 1988**

21. *Kate Vaiden*   **Reynolds Price**
Price's ninth novel is *Blue Calhoun*. In this one he fashions a twentieth-century Moll Flanders. Price creates wonderful female characters, but in his books they all suffer—big-time.
                                    306 pp.; 1986

22. *Family Linen*   **Lee Smith**
Smith is a favorite of reading clubs and her *Fair and Tender Ladies* and *The Devil's Dream* are both fine. As *Newsweek* said of this one, "Smith transmutes many of the elements of the Southern Gothic novel into farce, among them familial couplings and murder, feeble-minded cousins, loony aunts and lowdown tarts."   **291 pp.; 1985**

23. *Hall of Mirrors*   **Robert Stone**
The ultimate book with a New Orleans setting, Stone's first novel is the story of three drifters who are swept into town at the end of Mardi Gras and plunged into the seamy world of Louisiana politics.   **411 pp.; 1966**

24. *A Summons to Memphis*   Peter Taylor
The son of a widow is drawn from New York City into his
elder sisters' vendetta against their now dead father. He finds
that the central trauma of his life is his early dislocation from
Nashville to Memphis. This is Taylor's first novel in thirty-six
years.   **209 pp.; 1986**

25. *A Confederacy of Dunces*   John Kennedy Toole
Epic comedic novel about Ignatius J. Reilly, a thirty-year-old,
self-proclaimed genius in New Orleans who is out to reform
the entire twentieth century. This is the only novel by Toole,
who committed suicide at age thirty-two in 1969.
                                                 415 pp.; 1980

26. *The Optimist's Daughter*   Eudora Welty
Laurel Hand returns from Chicago to Mississippi after her
father's death and tries to come to terms with the small town
that he loved and what it means in her own life. *Losing Bat-
tles* and *Delta Wedding* are also recommended.
                                                 180 pp.; 1969

27. *Mama Makes Up Her Mind*   Bailey White
Subtitled *And Other Dangers of Southern Living*. Here are
fifty endearing true stories about rural South Georgia, where
the author lives and until recently taught first grade. Many of
them have been heard on National Public Radio's "All Things
Considered."   **240 pp.; 1993**

9

A JEWISH VIEW

1. *Free Agents*   Max Apple
A collection of winning short stories by the author of *Zip: A Novel of the Left and the Right*.   **197 pp.; 1984**

2. *Wartime Lies*   Louis Begley
First novel by a Manhattan lawyer who escaped the Nazis as a boy in Poland. Here the Jewish boy Maciek also survives, spends the war years in his aunt's care, and learns that deception saves *and* destroys.   **198 pp.; 1991**

3. *Seize the Day*   Saul Bellow
One day in the life of Tommy Wilhelm whose "spirit, the peculiar burden of his existence, lay upon him like an accretion, a load, a hump . . . of nameless things which it was the business of his life to carry about."   **118 pp.; 1956**

4. *The Book of J*   Harold Bloom and David Rosenberg
Scholars agree that the first strand in Genesis, Exodus, and Numbers was written by someone they call J, who lived in the tenth century. Using Rosenberg's new translation, Bloom asserts that this unknown writer was of Shakespeare's stature and was most probably a woman. *Some of us are not surprised.*   **340 pp.; 1990**

5. *Inherit the Mob*   Zev Chafets
So, Uncle Max dies, and what does his respectable journalist
nephew inherit? Nu, it's the last of the great American Jewish
gangs. Now that's, you should pardon the expression, Jewish
humor.   **312 pp.; 1991**

6. *The Goldin Boys*   Joseph Epstein
Stories by the noted essayist, set mostly in Chicago and
among Jews. Read *Pinto and Son* too.   **224 pp.; 1992**

7. *King of the Jews*   Leslie Epstein
Brilliant work of black humor, set in a small community in
Poland, this is the story of I. C. Trumpelmann, the director of
an orphanage no one wants to leave.   **352 pp.; 1993**

8. *The Provincials*   Eli N. Evans
Subtitled *A Personal History of Jews in the South*. Evans
records their history, from the early 1800s, when they fled the
northern ghettos, to the present. In spite of his effort to convince the reader that the "Jews were not aliens . . . but blood
and bones part of the South itself," *this* southern-born reader
is not entirely convinced. Read *The Lonely Days Were Sun-
days* too.   **331 pp.; 1973**

9. *Jews Without Money*   Michael Gold
This is the classic American urban proletariat novel. It documents that distinctive American experience, immigrant
poverty.   **234 pp.; 1930**

10. *Missing*   Michelle Herman
Rivke Vasilevsky, an eighty-nine-year-old widow, sits alone in
her Brooklyn apartment, remembering her past. While looking for her missing crystal beads she remembers her childhood in Poland, her marriage, her grandchildren, all the unre-
markable moments, and reconsiders their meaning.
                                               146 pp.; 1990

11. *The Painted Bird*   Jerzy Kosinski
One of the most disturbing books ever written, this is terror
and savagery as perpetrated against a dark-haired boy, either
a Jew or a gypsy, fleeing the Holocaust. Kosinski, who com-

mitted suicide, was the author of *Passion Play* and *Steps*, among others.   **251 pp.; 1965**

12. *Number the Stars*   Lois Lowry
A young adult book by a non-Jew, this tells the correct story of the Danish triumph in saving its Jewish citizens and dispels the myth of the Star of David supposedly worn by King Christian. The truth, however, is even more laudable and exemplary.   **137 pp.; 1989**

13. *The Assistant*   Bernard Malamud
A mundane environment, the small grocery store run by a poor Jew in a New York City borough, is the setting for a tale of oppression and the regenerative power of suffering. Provokes great discussions.   **297 pp.; 1957**

14. *The Shawl*   Cynthia Ozick
Includes a short story and a novella, *Rosa*. In "The Shawl" Rosa Lublin witnesses the murder of her infant daughter at the hands of a concentration camp guard. Thirty years later in *Rosa* she is "a madwoman and a scavenger," living in Florida. Powerful, required reading for everyone.

                                               70 pp.; 1983

15. *Later the Same Day*   Grace Paley
The third volume of wonderful stories about real people who struggle for meaning in their lives, written by the longtime antiwar, civil rights, and feminist activist. *The Little Disturbances of Man* and *Enormous Changes at the Last Minute* are equally good.   **211 pp.; 1985**

16. *Deborah, Golda, and Me*   Letty Cottin Pogrebin
Being Female and Jewish in America, the subtitle, pretty much sums it up; Pogrebin struggles here to reconcile her life as a Jew and a feminist. Great for discussion.   **400 pp.; 1991**

17. *The Rabbi in the Attic*   Eileen Pollack
Debut collection of funny stories concerning the dismissal of an obsessively Orthodox rabbi by his mildly Orthodox congregation.   **241 pp.; 1991**

18. *The Chosen*   **Chaim Potok**
Accessible picture of orthodox Jews in Brooklyn by the popular author of *My Name Is Asher Lev*.   **271 pp.; 1968**

19. *Solomon Gursky Was Here*   **Mordecai Richler**
The author, a Canadian Jew, writes here about a young scholar ruined by his obsession with a clan of Canadian Jewish bootleggers. Richler wrote *The Apprenticeship of Duddy Kravitz*, on which the movie was based.   **432 pp.; 1990**

20. *Lovingkindness*   **Anne Roiphe**
New York feminist faces her own conflicting feelings when her daughter decides to marry an Orthodox man in Israel and to become Orthodox herself. Great for discussion, even if you're not Jewish.   **279 pp.; 1987**

21. *The Counterlife*   **Philip Roth**
Nathan Zuckerman of *The Ghost Writer* (1979), *Zuckerman Unbound* (1981), and *The Anatomy Lesson* (1983) arrives in Israel. Roth plays on all the usual stereotypes in order to diffuse them.   **371 pp.; 1986**

22. *The Stories and Recollections*   **Umberto Saba**
       of Umberto Saba
Sketches and short stories about Jewish life in Trieste by an esteemed Italian writer who died in 1957.   **245 pp.; 1993**

23. *Scum*   **Isaac Bashevis Singer**
Controversial novel about the now rich and respectable Max, who revisits the scenes of his past on Krochmalna Street in Warsaw where he spent his past as a poverty-stricken youth.
                                                      218 pp.; 1991

24. *Writing Our Way Home*   **Ted Solotaroff and**
                                          Nessa Rapoport (editors)
Two dozen stories, all written since 1967, linked by the religious background of their authors and by the themes that often emerge in work by American Jews.   **380 pp.; 1992**

25. *Maus and Maus II,*   **Art Spiegelman**
  A Survivor's Tale
Two stories about Auschwitz survivors, Vladek and Anja
Spiegelman, told in comic book form. Winner of the Pulitzer
Prize Special Award. They should be read as one.

             159 pp.; 1986

26. *The Forgotten*   **Elie Wiesel**
Malkiel Rosenbaum's father persuades him to reexamine the
events of his father's wartime experiences in Romania fighting
the Nazis. With the help of the gravedigger, Hershel, he discovers another side to the stories.   **304 pp.; 1992**

27. *Bread Givers*   **Anzia Yezierska**
An autobiographical novel that condemns patriarchal Jewish
attitudes toward women, this is a look at the Jewish immigrant experience through a woman's eyes. Yezierska was born
in a mud hut on the Russian-Polish border. **297 pp.; 1925**

10

SAVE THE PLANET

1. *Desert Solitaire*   Edward Abbey
The famed environmentalist knew well how to step back
from the world in this nonfiction work in order to really see
it. *The Brave Cowboy* is a favorite of many western readers.
269 pp.; 1968

2. *A Natural History of the Senses*   Diane Ackerman
When you understand how you *see* the world, you will fight
to preserve it.   **331 pp.; 1990**

3. *Platte River*   Rick Bass
A petroleum geologist who lives on a remote ranch in northern Montana, here Bass has written three novellas that illumi-
nate mankind's relationship to the natural world. *Winter:
Notes from Montana* is a nonfiction book about a remote
valley of thirty inhabitants. *The Watch* is a collection of prize-
winning stories. Also great is *The Ninemile Wolves*, about the
reintroduction of those animals into the wild.   **224 pp.; 1994**

4. *Plain and Simple: A Woman's*   Sue Bender
   Journey to the Amish
Not strictly about the *physical* environment, but a good read
about an urban woman finding peace in the spiritual environment of the Amish in Iowa and Ohio.   **152 pp.; 1989**

5. *Natural Affairs*   **Peter Bernhardt**
The subtitle, *A Botanist Looks at the Attachments Between Plants and People*, says it all. One of the most interesting books I've read in a long time. Bernhardt also wrote *Wily Violets and Underground Orchids*.   **225 pp.; 1993**

6. *The Unsettling of America*   **Wendell Berry**
Subtitled *Culture and Agriculture*, this is Berry's personal, dramatic inquiry into the way we use the land that sustains us, and a vision of the future that includes a technologically controlled environment, damaged soil, and maximum production at any cost.   **228 pp.; 1977**

7. *The Crystal Desert*   **David G. Campbell**
A personal account of a remarkable place at the bottom of the world, the other Antarctica, the "banana belt" of the Antarctic Peninsula, and of its plants, rocks, and glaciers.
     308 pp.; 1992

8. *Silent Spring*   **Rachel Carson**
Probably the most influential book of the last fifty years, it documented in 1962 how the pesticide industry was destroying the natural world. Because of Carson, DDT was banned, and the environmental movement was launched. She also wrote *The Sea Around Us*, a bestseller.   **464 pp.; 1962**

9. *The Songlines*   **Bruce Chatwin**
This is a story of ideas. In an almost uninhabitable region of central Australia, where invisible pathways across the continent are known to us as songlines, two companions explore, among other questions, why man is the most restless and dissatisfied of animals. *In Patagonia* is, to say the least, about wandering and exile. Great for discussion.   **293 pp.; 1987**

10. *Pilgrim at Tinker Creek*   **Annie Dillard**
Winner of the 1974 Pulitzer Prize, this work reflects Dillard's urgent longing for a hidden God, for whom she searches in commonplace, natural events in her own neighborhood.
     271 pp.; 1974

11. *Earth in the Balance*   Al Gore
Gore is convinced that human civilization has brought us to the brink of catastrophe, and unless we rethink our relationship with nature the earth's ecology will be destroyed. Whatever your political persuasion, you should read this book!

407 pp.; 1992

12. *Land Circle*   Linda Hasselstrom
Subtitled *Writings Collected from the Land*, this book by an environmental writer and rancher offers some plainspoken insights on our connection with the land.   349 pp.; 1991

13. *A Country Year*   Sue Hubbell
Hubbell, a self-taught naturalist, took refuge for twelve years in the Missouri Ozarks and turned to commercial beekeeping to make a living. Rare and sweet.   221 pp.; 1986

14. *Animal Dreams*   Barbara Kingsolver
Flashbacks, dreams, Native American legends, and commitment to the earth by the author of *Pigs in Heaven*.

352 pp.; 1990

15. *Sand County Almanac*   Aldo Leopold
This book by a noted naturalist poses the question of "whether a still higher 'standard of living' is worth its cost in things natural, wild, and free. For us of the minority, the opportunity to see geese is more important than television, and the chance to find a pasque-flower is a right as inalienable as free speech." Leopold died fighting a grass fire on a neighbor's farm in 1948.   226 pp.; 1949

16. *Arctic Dreams*   Barry Lopez
Subtitled *Imagination and Desire In a Northern Landscape*, this is a celebration of the arctic landscape, of the animals who live there, and of some who have made the journey: Cook and Peary, sixth-century Irish monks, and Elizabethan sailors. Everything by Lopez is recommended: *Crow and Weasel, Desert Notes, Winter Count, Of Wolves and Men*, etc.   448 pp.; 1986

17. *Coming Into the Country*   **John McPhee**
Alaska, the last wilderness, is threatened, and McPhee travels
down an arctic river by kayak beyond the civilized frontiers
to tell us what we are about to lose.   **438 pp.; 1977**

18. *Bird of Life, Bird of Death*   **Jonathan Evan Maslow**
This naturalist and a photographer went to Guatemala in July
1983 to observe the quetzal, thought by many to be the most
beautiful bird in the hemisphere. For the bird of life the future
looks bleak, but the vulture, or zopilote, the bird of death, is
flourishing. Why? It feeds on the carrion provided by
Guatemala's political turmoil. Read *The Owl Papers* too.
240 pp.; 1986

19. *Gathering the Desert*   **Gary Paul Nabhan**
Wonderful study of the desert flora and ethnobiology of the
Sonoran Desert with a fine portrait of some of the Indians of
North America.   **209 pp.; 1985**

20. *The Island Within*   **Richard K. Nelson**
Nelson, an anthropologist, settled with his family in a small
town on the Pacific Northwest coast in order to explore a
nearby island. Instead he ended up exploring the meaning of
place itself and learning in the process about the wisdom of
Native Americans.   **304 pp.; 1991**

21. *Tales of the Earth*   **Charles Officer and Jake Page**
A geologist and a science writer warn of "instances of nature
making trouble for humanity and still others of humanity
making trouble for nature."   **226 pp.; 1993**

22. *Grizzly Years*   **Doug Peacock**
After Vietnam, Peacock crawled into the vastness of the
Rocky Mountain wilderness and met another veteran, the
American grizzly. Peacock has spent twenty years arguing
powerfully for the preservation of all things wild. We should
listen to him.   **288 pp.; 1990**

23. *Living by Water*   **Brenda Peterson**
Subtitled *Essays on Life, Land, and Spirit* and published in

Alaska. Peterson writes about aquatic biology, natural history, and ecology.   144 pp.; 1991

24. *Skywater*   Melinda Worth Popham

Many of the main characters here are coyotes, named after the trash that litters the desert. Poetic and important discussion, too, of the tailings from abandoned copper mines that have poisoned the groundwater. I love this book.

243 pp.; 1990

25. *Cadillac Desert*   Marc Reisner

This book documents the growth of the Bureau of Reclamation, responsible for Hoover, Shasta, and Grand Coulee dams, and its bitter rivalry with the U.S. Army Corps of Engineers. Neither pork barrel politics nor utopian schemes have yet solved the West's most relentless problem: water.

517 pp.; 1986

26. *Walden*   Henry David Thoreau

The greatest naturalist of them all ruminates about the change of seasons in a New England woods, nineteenth-century society, the good life, and—best of all—solitude.

207 pp.; 1854

27. *Refuge*   Terry Tempest Williams

An extraordinary book, hard to categorize, that is part memoir about the many women in her family who have died from cancers caused by irresponsible U.S. atomic testing in Utah, and part description, in this case of the flooded Bear River Migratory Bird Refuge near Great Salt Lake, and the emotional and physical impact of that phenomenon on the writer. Don't miss it.   304 pp.; 1991

28. *Run, River, Run*   Ann Zwinger

Zwinger is also the author of *Upcanyon, Downriver, A Naturalist's Journey.* Both books convince the reader of the power of firsthand experience and of honest description.

317 pp.; 1975

11

LET'S TALK ABOUT ME

Biography, Memoir, and Autobiography by Women

1. *The Bookmaker's Daughter* Shirley Abbott
The emphasis here is on Abbott's father, a promising scholar and avid reader, who was also a bookie and bootlegger, and her childhood in Hot Springs, Arkansas. **256 pp.; 1991**

2. *I Know Why the Caged Bird Sings* Maya Angelou
In the first part of a popular five-volume autobiography Angelou recalls life with her grandmother and racism in Arkansas. After she was raped by her mother's boyfriend when she was eight, she remained silent for five years. President Clinton chose his "fellow" Arkansan to read her poetry at his inauguration. **281 pp.; 1969**

3. *Spinster* Sylvia Ashton-Warner
This book focuses on issues of educational theory and racial understanding that grew out of the author's unorthodox method of teaching Maori children to read by using a "key" vocabulary. She was widely criticized in her native New Zealand, but the book sold well in the United States. **242 pp.; 1958**

4. *Writing Dangerously: Mary McCarthy and Her World* Carol Brightman

As Nancy Milford has written, this is the biography of "the pretty orphan from the West, the poor Catholic, ambitious Vassar girl who becomes the fatal woman of midcentury American letters." Includes the tale of her innumerable lovers and four husbands, including Edmund Wilson, with whom she had a tempestuous marriage.   714 pp.; 1992

5. *Black Ice*   Lorene Carey

Life as a black student at the exclusive (and formerly all-white and male) St. Paul's School in Concord, New Hampshire.   256 pp.; 1991

6. *The Road From Coorain*   Jill Ker Conway

A great favorite of reading groups, this is the memoir of an Australian who grew up to be an American college president.   256 pp.; 1989

7. *Memoirs of a Dutiful Daughter*   Simone de Beauvoir

The autobiography of the fascinating woman who wrote *The Second Sex*, loved Sartre, and changed the way we all think about gender.   360 pp.; 1959

8. *An American Childhood*   Annie Dillard

This is the Pulitzer Prize–winning author's vivid, moving memoir of growing up in Pittsburgh in the 1950s.   255 pp.; 1987

9. *The North China Lover*   Marguerite Duras

Set in Vietnam, this novel began as notes for the movie *The Lover*, about a French girl, probably Duras, obsessed with a Chinese man.   128 pp.; 1992

10. *A Romantic Education*   Patricia Hampl

An evocation of the author's Czech heritage that blends the personal and the historical.   344 pp.; 1981

11. *Lost in Translation*   Eva Hoffman

When Hoffman emigrated at thirteen from Poland to Vancouver, she lost her language, her culture, and her footing. This intellectual's version of the classic immigrant success story is the final step in her reanchoring.   **288 pp.; 1988**

12. *In My Place*   **Charlayne Hunter-Gault**
The national correspondent for "The MacNeil/Lehrer Newshour" reflects on her childhood and young adulthood and on her historic role as one of two black students who desegregated the University of Georgia in 1961.   **192 pp.; 1993**

13. *When Heaven and Earth Changed Places*   Le Ly Hyslip
Award-winning account of the author's youth in wartime Vietnam; followed by *Child of War, Woman of Peace*, which explains how a peasant woman, twice widowed, lives through rape, poverty, and desertion and ends up worth more than a million dollars.   **374 pp.; 1989**

14. *The Woman Warrior*   **Maxine Hong Kingston**
Subtitled *Memoirs of a Girlhood Among Ghosts*, this won the National Book Critics Circle Award for nonfiction; it contains Kingston's autobiography, recounts the evolution of her Asian-American identity, and remains one of the most influential and widely read books by an American woman in the late twentieth century. A must.   **209 pp.; 1977**

15. *Road Song*   **Natalie Kusz**
In 1969 Kusz and her family packed up the car and headed for Alaska. They ended up a hundred miles from Fairbanks, with temperatures of sixty below. Then disaster struck.
                258 pp.; 1990

16. *Secret Ceremonies*   **Deborah Laake**
A woman's memories of being raised a Mormon, the unhappy marriages that ensued, and her life now as a Jack, or lapsed, Mormon in Phoenix. Face it, we're all fascinated with secret church ceremonies.   **240 pp.; 1993**

17. *Memories of a Catholic Girlhood*   Mary McCarthy
McCarthy was raised by relatives after both parents died in 1918; this book recounts the severe, rigid Catholicism that dominated her emotionally deprived childhood. In any case

she grew up to write *The Group* and a large output of fiction and nonfiction.   245 pp.; 1957

18. *Anne Sexton: A Biography*   Diane Wood Middlebrook
National Book Award for 1991. A definitive examination of the poet and her life that uses therapy session tapes to round out the picture. Even if you're not interested in poetry, you'll like this one.   448 pp.; 1990

19. *Silent Dancing: A Partial*   Judith Ortiz-Cofer
    Remembrance of a Puerto Rican Childhood
Recipient of a PEN citation and a Pushcart Prize, Cofer talks about how females are conditioned and the price of that lesson.   168 pp.; 1990

20. *Johnny's Girl*   Kim Rich
Subtitled *A Daughter's Memoir of Growing Up in Alaska's Underworld*. Rich is a journalist whose father, Johnny Rich, Jr., was a well-known mobster in Anchorage. Her mother was a former stripper who died the year before he was murdered.
                                    288 pp.; 1993

21. *Journal of a Solitude*   May Sarton
Inner and outer worlds, daily life in New Hampshire, and the solace of silence.   208 pp.; 1973

22. *The Four of Us*   Elizabeth Swados
The gifted composer chronicles the ways in which her schizophrenic, self-destructive brother dominated her family. The book is divided into four sections, each focusing on a different family member.   243 pp.; 1991

Biography, Memoir, and Autobiography by Men

1. *Dickens*   Peter Ackroyd
Very long work on the unique figure of Charles Dickens. More mystery and intrigue than you would imagine from reading *A Christmas Carol*.   1,195 pp.; 1991

2. *Days of Grace*   **Arthur Ashe and Arnold Rampersad**
The recollections of the great tennis champion reflect the courage needed for his triumph on the tennis court, his survival as a black man in America, and his confrontation with death as a casualty of AIDS, contracted through a defective blood transfusion during heart surgery.   **441 pp.; 1993**

3. *Growing Up Latino*   **Harold Augenbraum and Ilan Stavans (editors)**
Memoirs and stories by people of Latin background; all reflections on life in the United States.   **344 pp.; 1993**

4. *Coming Up Down Home*   **Cecil Brown**
Subtitled *A Memoir of a Southern Childhood*, and by the author of *The Life and Loves of Mr. Jiveass Nigger*, this is an engrossing memoir of childhood in the small farming village of Bolton, North Carolina.   **256 pp.; 1993**

5. *Talking at the Gates*   **James Campbell**
The black homosexual writer James Baldwin found life in these United States a trial. He lived in Paris for much of his life, and this biographer, who knew him, combines the factual with the subjective.   **288 pp.; 1991**

6. *The Journals of John Cheever*   **John Cheever**
This is the writer's life from the late 1940s to his death from cancer in 1982, including his twenty-year battle with chronic alcoholism, his hidden homosexuality, and his many affairs with women. Read his daughter Susan's memoir, *Home Before Dark*, too.   **399 pp.; 1991**

7. *Learning to Bow*   **Bruce S. Feiler**
Not exactly a memoir, but a fascinating account of teaching English for one year to junior high school students in Sano, Japan. Feiler takes a ritual outdoor bath; his students learn the High Five handshake.   **322 pp.; 1991**

8. *Pack My Bag: A Self-Portrait*   **Henry Green**
Originally published in Britain, this is pretty much all that is known of a very enigmatic novelist, revered in some writerly circles, who lived from 1905 to 1973.   **242 pp.; 1940**

9. *The Autobiography of Malcolm X as Told to Alex Haley*
The story of the civil rights leader, former Muslim, and failed small-time hood, now an icon to many. There are millions of copies in print.   **608 pp.; 1965**

10. *Life Work*   Donald Hall
The very ill poet writes here what the *New York Times* calls "a brief, dense, painful, and memorable book . . . a notable contribution to our strange new genre, autothanatography."
                                                      124 pp.; 1993

11. *Trollope: A Biography*   N. Jon Hall
Trollope wrote sixty novels in a long life, and he was in all ways an outstanding personality. Hall does a great job with the life *and* the work.   **600 pp.; 1991**

12. *Albums of Early Life*   Stanley Kauffmann
Here we meet Kauffmann, film and theater critic, as farm-hand, drama school prodigy, young lover, comic-book writer, playwright, and more.   **229 pp.; 1980**

13. *A Different Person*   James Merrill
Son of the man who gave his name to the world's largest bro-kerage firm, the famed poet discloses how he journeyed to Italy and, with the help of a good psychiatrist, made peace with his homosexuality and began to write.   **271 pp.; 1993**

14. *Salem Is My Dwelling Place*   Edwin Haviland Miller
Subtitled *A Life of Nathaniel Hawthorne*. Miller looks for the secrets in Hawthorne's life but finds instead the essence of nineteenth-century America in Massachusetts.   **648 pp.; 1991**

15. *Becoming a Man*   Paul Monette
Subtitled *Half a Life Story*, this National Book Award winner chronicles Monette's struggle to finally accept his homosexu-ality.   **288 pp.; 1992**

16. *If I Die in a Combat Zone,*   Tim O'Brien
    Box Me Up and Ship Me Home
The Phi Beta Kappa, summa cum laude graduate of Macalester College and author of *Waiting for Cacciato* tries

to make sense of the experience of serving in Vietnam as a foot soldier. He won the Purple Heart in action near My Lai.

199 pp.; 1973

17. *Randall Jarrell: A Literary Life*   **William H. Pritchard**
A very good critic describes the life and explains the work of a very unusual poet.

338 pp.; 1990

18. *What Did I Do?*   **Larry Rivers**
Outrageous and uncensored portrait of the artist's often perverse life as part of the art, jazz, and literary worlds in postwar New York.

512 pp.; 1993

19. *Hunger of Memory*   **Richard Rodriguez**
A Chicano essayist born in San Francisco, Rodriguez wrote this autobiographical account of his education and search for identity. His second book was *Mexico's Children*.

195 pp.; 1982

20. *Up from Slavery*   **Booker T. Washington**
Freed from slavery at the age of eight, Washington managed by 1872 to gain entrance to Hampton Institute, from which he graduated in 1876. One of the founders of Tuskegee Institute, this extraordinary man had a profound influence upon the Americans of his day.

330 pp.; 1900

21. *The Duke of Deception*   **Geoffrey Wolff**
Wolff recounts life with his father, a confidence man— "bright, quick, musical, charming, a wonderful storyteller" and "also a bullshit artist who doctored his bloodline and fabricated his *curriculum vitae*, becoming the man he felt he should have been rather than the man his history had made." Also *A Day at the Beach*, essays of recollection.

275 pp.; 1979

22. *This Boy's Life*   **Tobias Wolff**
Flannery O'Connor said that anybody who survived his childhood had enough to write about for the rest of his life. In Wolff's case that includes the separation from his father and brother, wandering with his mother from Florida to Washing-

ton State, and life with a Dickensian stepfather. Read his two collections of short stories, *Back in the World* and *In the Garden of the North American Martyrs*, too.   **288 pp.; 1989**

23. *Black Boy*   **Richard Wright**
The years pass, but this remains an unforgettable story of growing up in the Jim Crow South. Wright is one of America's most powerful writers.   **528 pp.; 1945**

12

AFRICAN-AMERICAN
IMAGES AND IDEAS

1. *Going to Meet the Man*   **James Baldwin**
This collection of short stories includes "Sonny's Blues." *The Fire Next Time* (1963) grew from a long magazine essay on the Black Muslims and the civil rights struggle.

249 pp.; 1965

2. *Gorilla, My Love*   **Toni Cade Bambara**
First collection of short stories followed by *The Sea Birds Are Still Alive*, and *The Salt Eaters*, which includes the widely anthologized "My Man Bovanne."   **177 pp.; 1972**

3. *Your Blues Ain't Like Mine*   **Bebe Moore Campbell**
This novel recalls the racially motivated murder of Emmett Till, a black teenager killed for whistling at a white woman in Mississippi in 1955. The killer's family and the victim's family are inextricably linked by this act.   **352 pp.; 1992**

4. *Good Times*   **Lucille Clifton**
This collection and *Good News About the Earth*, both by the Maryland poet, optimistically portray the value of the family and the ghetto as home. Read *Generations* too.

85 pp.; 1969

5. *Notes of a Hanging Judge*   **Stanley Crouch**
A collection of essays by the well-known social critic who
makes a lot of sense on the subject of racism. His new novel is
First Snow in Kokomo.   **296 pp.; 1990**

6. *1959*   **Thulani Davis**
Coming-of-age story by the well-known playwright, poet,
and journalist, set against the beginnings of the civil rights
movement.   **304 pp.; 1991**

7. *Invisible Man*   **Ralph Ellison**
Ellison won the National Book Award for this novel and created a new mode of fiction by combining social realism with
elements of surrealism. This is arguably the most distinguished American work of its time.   **429 pp.; 1953**

8. *Divine Days*   **Leon Forrest**
New masterpiece that takes place on the South Side of
Chicago over seven days in late February 1966. The narrator,
Joubert Jones, is a playwright who plans to write about
Sugar-Groove, a Mississippi half-caste who has disappeared.
Don't miss this one.   **1,138 pp.; 1993**

9. *Praying for Sheetrock*   **Melissa Fay Greene**
Intimate reporting about a black community in rural Georgia
that moved from passivity to civil rights militancy to calm.
       352 pp.; 1991

10. *Their Eyes Were Watching God*   **Zora Neale Hurston**
Classic of black literature, this is the story of a strong-spirited
woman's quest for love and self-fulfillment. Read Hurston's
autobiography, *Dust Tracks on the Road*, as well.
       286 pp.; 1937

11. *Middle Passage*   **Charles Johnson**
Winner of the National Book Award, this novel is about an
emancipated and very educated slave who stows away on a
ship bound for Africa.   **160 pp.; 1990**

12. *Lost in the City: Stories*   **Edward P. Jones**
For this collection of fourteen stories of African-American life

in Washington, D.C., Jones won the PEN/Hemingway Award and was nominated for the National Book Award.

256 pp.; 1992

13. *The Avenue Clayton City*   C. Eric Lincoln
Dedicated "To Alex Haley, a Late Installment on an Old Promise," this is an evocative novel about a prototypical southern town languishing between the First and and Second World Wars. "The Avenue" is the main street in Clayton City, but it is an unpaved road with no gutters on the black end of town.   288 pp.; 1988

14. *Waiting to Exhale*   Terry McMillan
Bestselling novel of four African-American women who are waiting to exhale when (and if) they *finally* meet their misters right! In spite of *Exhale*'s huge success, many readers prefer *Disappearing Acts*.   416 pp.; 1992

15. *Daddy Was a Number Runner*   Louise Meriwether
This was the first African-American novel to assess the effects of the Depression on a black family, and it is a true picture of the poverty and despair of the ghetto. Should be required reading everywhere.   208 pp.; 1970

16. *Playing in the Dark*   Toni Morrison
The Nobel Prize–winning author calls for literary scholarship that will help all Americans understand how black experience is interwoven in American literature.   91 pp.; 1993

17. *Scorpions*   William Dean Myers
Myers has written over forty books, primarily about blacks in the inner city. This one won the Newberry. *Fallen Angels*, about life and death in Vietnam, was in part inspired by his brother's death there on his first day of service. *The Righteous Revenge of Artemis Bonner* is a picaresque tale set in the Wild West.   216 pp.; 1988

18. *The Women of Brewster Place*   Gloria Naylor
Seven women end up on a blind alley leading into a dead-end street, but their spirits and stories are anything but impover-

ished. Her latest book is *Bailey's Cafe*, following *Linden Hills* and *Mama Day*.   **192 pp.; 1982**

19. *The Street*   **Ann Petry**
An American classic and a historical document about violent and impoverished life in the city, especially for a woman trying to raise a son. Petry is the author of *Miss Muriel and Other Stories*.   **436 pp.; 1946**

20. *High Cotton*   **Darryl Pinckney**
A dense, rich first novel about an alienated but well-educated and nonconformist black man, who is obsessed with racial identities.   **320 pp.; 1992**

21. *All-Bright Court*   **Connie Porter**
In this first novel Porter describes twenty years in the lives of the black residents of a housing project in the shadow of Buffalo's steel mills. Watch this writer.   **240 pp.; 1991**

22. *Betsey Brown*   **Ntozake Shange**
The story of a thirteen-year-old girl, poised between the enchantment of childhood and the possibilities of adulthood. Set in St. Louis in 1957, the story reveals the effects of both racism and integration. Shange, a playwright, is the author of *for colored girls who have considered suicide/when the rainbow is enuf*.   **196 pp.; 1985**

23. *The Content of Our Character*   **Shelby Steele**
Subtitled *A New Vision of Race in America*. Steele argues that it is time for blacks to stop thinking of themselves as victims. This position did not endear him to some members of the Left but ensured his celebrity on the Right and gave everyone in the middle plenty to think about.   **175 pp.; 1990**

24. *I Been in Sorrow's Kitchen and*   **Susan Straight**
    Licked Out All the Pots
Like all good writers, Straight misses nothing in her portrait of Marietta Cook, born in the Gullah-speaking Low Country of South Carolina. She ends up among the luxury condomini-

ums and freeways in the promised land of California. Straight
wrote *Aquaboogie*.   **355 pp.; 1992**

25. *The Color Purple*   Alice Walker
Epistolary novel in which the sisters Celie and Nettie epitomize the friendship black women must have with each other
in the face of the oppression they face in their relationships
with black men and whites in general. Don't miss this book;
even the movie was great.   **253 pp.; 1982**

26. *Jubilee*   Margaret Walker
Music is the leitmotif in this novel about Elvira Ware Brown,
called Vyry, one of fifteen children and a slave in nineteenth-
century America. She was the actual great-grandmother of the
author. Unforgettable. Walker is best known for her first
book, *For My People* (1942).   **497 pp.; 1966**

27. *Dessa Rose*   Sherley Anne Williams
In this novel Williams challenges the accuracy of the black
female experience as portrayed in William Styron's *Confes-
sions of Nat Turner*. She is also an award-winning poet.
                                                    236 pp.; 1986

13

THE IMPACT OF ILLNESS

1. *The Savage God*　　　　　　　　　　　**A. Alvarez**
Alvarez was the first writer on the subject of depression and suicide who moved me deeply. Read this book together with William Styron's chronicle of his own descent into mental illness.　　　　　　　　　　　　　　　　　**299 pp.; 1972**

2. *Tender Mercies*　　　　　　　　　　　**Rosellen Brown**
In anyone else's hands, the story of a man who runs over his wife with a motorboat, and her subsequent lifetime paralysis, would be a plot for a trash novel. Here it is a splendid examination of a fight for survival and of an imperfect marriage that is tested to the extreme.　　　　　　　**259 pp.; 1978**

3. *Anatomy of an Illness*　　　　　　　　**Norman Cousins**
The book is a fuller version of an article first published in 1976 in the *New England Journal of Medicine* about the partnership between a physician and a patient in battling illness, and the holistic idea that the human mind and body are a single entity. Cousins was the editor of the *Saturday Review* for more than thirty years.　　　　　　　　**160 pp.; 1979**

4. *The Broken Cord*　　　　　　　　　　**Michael Dorris**
Fetal Alcohol Syndrome, an incurable but *preventable* birth defect from which Dorris's first adopted son suffered, is what

often results when pregnant women drink. Should be required reading for every potential parent in America, not just those from the author's own Native American culture.

300 pp.; 1989

5. *An Autobiography*   **Janet Frame**
Gathered here are *To the Is-land*, *Angel at My Table*, and *Envoy from Mirror City*. New Zealand's greatest novelist was misdiagnosed as schizophrenic and spent eight years in a mental hospital. She was saved from brain surgery not by a doctor's epiphany but by winning a literary prize for her first book, written before her commitment in 1945.

400 pp.; 1991

6. *At the Will of the Body*   **Arthur W. Frank**
This is a meditative reflection on illness by a man who suffered a heart attack at thirty-nine and cancer at forty. Great for discussions. .

144 pp.; 1991

7. *The Yellow Wallpaper and*   **Charlotte Perkins Gilman**
   Other Writings
Autobiographical title story of depression following childbirth and the typical mistreatment by a Philadelphia neurologist. The fictional narrator goes mad; Gilman saved herself and went on to write ten more books, including *Herland*.

63 pp.; 1892

8. *I Never Promised You a Rose Garden*   **Hannah Green**
Novel about a sixteen-year-old girl who retreats from reality into psychosis, and her struggle, aided by a knowledgeable psychiatrist, to reenter the world after three years in a mental hospital.

256 pp.; 1964

9. *We Have Always Lived in the Castle*   **Shirley Jackson**
In this unusual novel Jackson traces how the female psyche is rendered sociopathic. She wrote "The Lottery."

214 pp.; 1962

10. *Girl, Interrupted*   **Susanna Kaysen**
Written by the daughter of a famous scientist. This is the tri-

umphantly funny story of an almost two-year stay at McLean
Hospital, a psychiatric institution in Belmont, Massachusetts,
beginning in 1967.   **168 pp.; 1993**

11. *Sailing*   **Susan Kenney**
A beautiful, even hopeful, semiautobiographical novel about
the impact of incurable cancer on a marriage and the courage
needed for the family's survival.   **320 pp.; 1988**

12. *ANNA: A Daughter's Life*   **William Loizeaux**
After the author's five-and-a-half-month-old daughter died
from VATER syndrome, a rare condition involving congenital
deformities of the heart, kidney, and esophagus, he began to
write this intimate journal.   **224 pp.; 1992**

13. *Notes from the Border*   **Jane Taylor McDonnell**
Searingly honest account of raising a high-functioning autistic
child, Paul, who wrote the Afterword, but who remains in a
kind of emotional no-man's-land, intensely self-conscious of
his difference.   **384 pp.; 1993**

14. *Ordinary Time*   **Nancy Mairs**
As in *Plaintext*, *Remembering the Bone House*, and *Carnal
Acts*, the essays here share the difficulties of a marriage and a
life compounded by Mairs's multiple sclerosis and bouts of
depression. She is a Christian with an extraordinary capacity
for devotion, but her work stands conventional devotional literature on its head.   **238 pp.; 1993**

15. *The Art Lover*   **Carole Maso**
Caroline, the protagonist, is on a search for clues about how
to live. When Maso breaks the fictive form with a harrowing
account of her friend Gary Falk's death from AIDS, the novel
becomes a testament to redemption. Unique evocation of fictional and real pain.   **243 pp.; 1990**

16. *Family Pictures*   **Sue Miller**
Story of a large Chicago family dominated by the autism of
one child, Randall, and of the attendant stresses on a marriage.   **389 pp.; 1990**

17. *Halfway Home*   Paul Monette

Love in the face of AIDS in a timely and affecting story.

262 pp.; 1991

18. *The English Patient*   Michael Ondaatje

Four dissimilar people who suffer from the physical and emotional damages of World War II meet in a deserted Italian villa. Complex, haunting interior monologues. This novel won the Booker Prize.   307 pp.; 1992

19. *The Bell Jar*   Sylvia Plath

In this American poet's semiautobiographical account, Esther Greenwood, a talented writer, suffers from society's frequent dismissal of the female artist.   296 pp.; 1971

20. *Patrimony: A True Story*   Philip Roth

A very fine writer brings his storytelling powers to his father's struggle with a fatal brain tumor. At times the book is even funny.   238 pp.; 1991

21. *The Man Who Mistook*   Oliver Sacks
    His Wife for a Hat

By the author of *Awakenings*, which presented the life stories of twenty patients afflicted by an extraordinary disease. Here Sacks explores a greater variety of neurological disorders and their effects upon the minds and lives of the patients.

223 pp.; 1985

22. *Life Size*   Jenefer Shute

Searing first novel that describes the inner life of a sixty-seven-pound, anorexic, hospitalized young woman who rages against treatment. Don't miss this one.   230 pp.; 1992

23. *Illness as Metaphor*   Susan Sontag

Sontag's point is that illness is *not* a metaphor, and that the best way to confront illness is to resist metaphoric thinking. She cites images and metaphors of illness from medical and psychiatric thinking and from the greatest works of literature.

88 pp.; 1978

24. *Darkness Visible: A Memoir of Madness*   William Styron

Several years ago, this author of *Lie Down in Darkness* and *Sophie's Choice* was overtaken by despair. His real healers, he said, were "seclusion and time."   **84 pp.; 1990**

25. *Miss Lonelyhearts*   Nathanael West

Unusual novel about a newspaperman, so named because he has been assigned to write the agony column and to answer the letters from Desperate, Sick-of-It-All, and Disillusioned. *The Day of the Locust* is also by West.   **185 pp.; 1933**

14

DON'T-MISS NINETEENTH-CENTURY NOVELS

1. *Little Women and Good Wives*   Louisa May Alcott
Originally published in two parts: the first half introduces Jo,
Meg, Amy, and Beth and the overperfect Marmee; in the second part Beth dies and Jo marries. Repeat after me: This is
not a children's book; this is not a children's book; this is . . .
                                        643 pp.; 1868–69

2. *Emma*   Jane Austen
Austen's dates are 1775–1817, but since she is generally considered the greatest English novelist, her best novel—with her
most successful heroine, Emma Woodhouse—is included
here.   378 pp.; 1816

3. *Looking Backward*   Edward Bellamy
In late nineteenth-century America Bellamy laid bare the
social inequities and offered the reforms that would lead to a
utopian society. Your reading group might combine this with
other utopian novels (*Erewhon* by Samuel Butler) or
dystopias (antiutopian novels) like George Orwell's *1984*.
                                        234 pp.; 1888

4. *Jane Eyre*   Charlotte Brontë

No one is truly educated without reading this one. Mr. Rochester has become an archetypal figure, and then, of course, there's the madwoman in the attic.   **434 pp.; 1847**

5. *Wuthering Heights*   Emily Brontë

Here are the Byronic Heathcliff and the romantic Cathy in the multilayered and ever-fresh story of two disparate British families in an isolated, harsh, and beautiful environment.

298 pp.; 1847

6. *The Way of All Flesh*   Samuel Butler

A few years beyond 1900, but this novel belongs on this list. Butler describes parent-child relationships during the Victorian era, using several generations of the Pontifex family, who bred maladjusted, introverted children.   **423 pp.; 1903**

7. *The Leatherstocking Tales*   J. Fenimore Cooper

The Pioneers (1823), *The Last of the Mohicans* (1826), *The Pathfinder* (1840), *The Deerslayer* (1841), and ending, narratively, with *The Prairie* (1827), the closing chapter in the great American saga of the frontiersman Natty Bumppo and his Indian friend Chingachgook.   **402 pp.; 1823–41**

8. *Bleak House*   Charles Dickens

Considering the current view of lawyers in the United States, the lawsuit between Jarndyce and Jarndyce, based on "another well-known suit in Chancery, not yet decided, which was commenced before the close of the last century and in which more than double the amount of seventy thousand pounds has been swallowed up in costs," is contemporary reading at its best. My favorite of the Dickens novels.

808 pp.; 1852–53

9. *The Adventures of Sherlock Holmes*   Arthur Conan Doyle

The pipe, the cape, and Watson—all part of the milieu of the ultimate British detective. He is available to a whole new generation on PBS's "Mystery Theatre."   **279 pp.; 1892**

10. *The Mill on the Floss* George Eliot
Probably the most widely read novel by the author of *Middle-march*; here Maggie Tulliver leads a dull life and cares for her largely worthless and unlikable brother. Great for discussions about responsibility and denial.   595 pp.; 1860

11. *The Damnation of Theron Ware* Harold Frederic
I had to read this one in graduate school, but I'm glad now. (And no one will ever beat you on a trivia test after *you* read it!) An exposé of the cultural barrenness of the American small town, this is the ancestor of *Main Street* and *Elmer Gantry*.   287 pp.; 1896

12. *Mary Barton, A Tale of* Elizabeth Gaskell
    Manchester Life
British working-class life and a recession in an industrial town. Good picture of the then-nascent trade unions.
    487 pp.; 1848

13. *The New Grub Street* George Gissing
Autobiographical work about the effects of poverty on the freedom of the writer. Gissing rebelled against Victorian society and had a wretched life but left us this very fine novel.
    543 pp.; 1891

14. *Jude the Obscure* Thomas Hardy
In my opinion, Hardy's best (and last) novel about the short and miserable life of a man thwarted by fate, weakness, and society. Don't miss it.   493 pp.; 1895

15. *The Scarlet Letter* Nathaniel Hawthorne
Hester Prynne wears the "A" for adultery; her lover, the minister, is ruined by his hidden guilt, and her husband goes nuts—all in seventeenth-century America.   283 pp.; 1850

16. *Daisy Miller* Henry James
The most popular of James's novels. Here his usual American innocents in Europe are represented by the truly blemishless and sympathetic Daisy. If you find James boring, as many readers do, choose this one.   83 pp.; 1878

17. *The Country of the Pointed Firs* Sarah Orne Jewett
Usually considered a New England regional realist, Jewett has a preference for the rural that is always obvious. Women are central in her work, which is definitely worth reading.
306 pp.; 1896

18. *McTeague: A Story of San Francisco* Frank Norris
Norris died at thirty-two following an operation but left this story of a sado-masochistic marriage, featuring, of all people, a dentist as hero. (He ends up, by the way—for those of us who have had root canal—chained to a corpse in the middle of Death Valley.)
324 pp.; 1881

19. *The Story of an African Farm* Olive Shreiner
In her only nonposthumous novel, Shreiner yearns for a life beyond that offered by South African colonialism; she rejects Victorian materialism and spiritual dryness. Shreiner, an antiracist and anti-imperialist writer who died in 1920, is a central figure in modern white South African literature.
375 pp.; 1883

20. *Dr. Jekyll and Mr. Hyde* Robert Louis Stevenson
Classic romantic adventure based on the dual personalities of a single man representing beauty and the beast.
62 pp.; 1886

21. *Uncle Tom's Cabin* Harriet Beecher Stowe
Subtitled *Life Among the Lowly*, this novel, in spite of its impossibly good and/or evil characters, greatly raised the public consciousness about slavery. If you get to Hartford, Connecticut, visit Stowe's house; she lived next door to Mark Twain.
116 pp.; 1852

22. *Vanity Fair* William Makepeace Thackeray
The prototype of all climbers, Becky Sharp is a witty, clever, accomplished young woman who is determined to break into fashionable society by any means possible. You could read this one in the Hamptons (while eating a three-dollar blueberry muffin), for example!
754 pp.; 1847

23. *Phineas Finn*   **Anthony Trollope**

An Irish political boss loses his beloved and rejects the hand and fortune of a rich widow. Good way to understand nineteenth-century Irish politics. *Barchester Towers* is the novel with the odious chaplain Mr. Slope. *He Knew He Was Right* is the usual academic favorite.   **367 pp.; 1869**

24. *Huckleberry Finn*   **Mark Twain**

Sequel to the *Adventures of Tom Sawyer*, this is a more somber and polished novel. The Mississippi River as time and possibility, friendship between a man and a boy, and lighting out for the territory—all themes in American literature—were born here.   **435 pp.; 1884**

15

EARLY TWENTIETH-CENTURY WRITING

1. *Winesburg, Ohio*   **Sherwood Anderson**
Still holds up as an examination of the many grotesques in small-town America, always struggling as individuals against the norms of society.   **303 pp.; 1919**

2. *Death of the Heart*   **Elizabeth Bowen**
The vulnerability of the orphaned Portia in this novel recalls Bowen's own insecure childhood, "motherless since [she] was thirteen," "shuttling between two countries: Ireland and England," an outsider everywhere.   **418 pp.; 1938**

3. *The Professor's House*   **Willa Cather**
The greatest American author to have written about the prairies, populated at the end of the nineteenth century and early twentieth century by Norwegians, Swedes, Bohemians, and Germans. Here a scholarly professor in a midwestern university is approaching old age; the subplot concerns the Cliff Dwellers in the Southwest. Also *A Lost Lady*, *My Mortal Enemy*, and *O Pioneers!*   **283 pp.; 1925**

4. *Men and Wives*   **Ivy Compton-Burnett**
The story of a Victorian family dominated by the archetypal maternal power figure, Harriet Haslam.   **288 pp.; 1931**

5. *Lord Jim* **Joseph Conrad**
One of Conrad's major themes is the fragility of the bonds that hold an individual to society. In this adventure story Jim is involved in the disgraceful affair of the *Patna* and its pilgrim passengers. **417 pp.; 1900**

6. *The Enormous Room* **e. e. cummings**
Autobiographical novel set in the filthy jail where he was imprisoned, and where the captors are worse than their prisoners. Read *A Pilgrim's Progress* at the same time.
271 pp.; 1922

7. *As I Lay Dying* **William Faulkner**
Don't be afraid of the multivoiced stream-of-consciousness technique, as the Burden family carries Addie's coffin to her hometown for burial. By any standards, this short novel is a not-to-be-missed masterpiece. **250 pp.; 1930**

8. *Tender Is the Night* **F. Scott Fitzgerald**
The wife who becomes her psychiatrist husband's patient is, of course, based on Fitzgerald's mentally ill wife, Zelda. More autobiography surfaces in *This Side of Paradise*.
349 pp.; 1934

9. *Howards End* **E. M. Forster**
One of the great laserlike looks at personal and social relationships among the upper classes in Britain. If you haven't written your will already, read this first. **393 pp.; 1919**

10. *In This Our Life* **Ellen Glasgow**
In this Pulitzer Prize–winning book Glasgow advocates some experimentation with sexual relationships, far removed from the mores of her old colonial Virginia family. **467 pp.; 1941**

11. *Brave New World* **Aldous Huxley**
Prophetic look at the problems of genetic engineering. You might combine this with the reading of a more updated anti-utopian novel like *The Giver*, by Lois Lowry. **288 pp.; 1958**

12. *A Portrait of the Artist as a Young Man* **James Joyce**
These connected stories of a boy's childhood in Catholic

Dublin form a central work in modern literature. Also
Dubliners.   **299 pp.; 1916**

13. *The Rainbow* and *Women in Love*   D. H. Lawrence
These are Lawrence's best novels, in spite of the fact that an
entire generation of readers hid *Lady Chatterley's Lover*
under the socks. (Or was it the mattress?) A fine look at
young married life.   *The Rainbow*: **467 pp.; 1915**
                              Women in Love: **464 pp.; 1920**

14. *Babbitt*   Sinclair Lewis
The title has entered the language to represent the small-town
businessman who is consumed by his own materialism and
social climbing.   **898 pp.; 1923**

15. *Of Human Bondage*   F. Somerset Maugham
Maugham is a great storyteller usually derided by literary
critics. This is his most important and autobiographical
novel—about a handicapped boy and his life as an artist.
                                            648 pp.; 1915

16. *Flowering Judas and*   Katherine Anne Porter
   Other Stories
Many of Porter's stories (all better than *Ship of Fools*) focus
on the moment of epiphany when women realize that they
have often been deluded about their lives. "The Jilting of
Granny Weatherall" is a particular favorite.   **285 pp.; 1935**

17. *The Catherine Wheel*   Jean Stafford
The struggle in Stafford's work is always between spiritual
and/or sexual death, on the one hand, and the demands of
culture and society, on the other.   **281 pp.; 1925**

18. *The Grapes of Wrath*   John Steinbeck
A Pulitzer Prize winner, this novel expresses Steinbeck's con-
cern for the poverty and hopelessness of those driven from
their homes by the Depression—like the Joads who migrate
from Oklahoma to California. Steinbeck's sympathy was with
the agricultural workers of the then decidedly non–Golden
State.   **619 pp.; 1939**

19. *The Custom of the Country*   **Edith Wharton**
The current favorite of Wharton scholars, this pits an American fortune hunter, the insatiably ambitious and beautiful Undine Spragg from Apex, Kansas, against the European aristocracy. Unusual in that Wharton uses a woman to represent materialism and greed.   370 pp.; 1913

20. *The Judge*   **Rebecca West**
Born Cecily Isabel Fairfield in Ireland, West took the name of Ibsen's heroine in *Rosmershalm*. This novel explores two generations of the women's suffrage movement.   430 pp.; 1922

21. *Mrs. Dalloway*   **Virginia Woolf**
While Clarissa Dalloway plans her dinner party, with all the accoutrements of her social class and status, Septimus Smith, emotionally damaged by World War I, draws closer to suicide. One of modernism's greatest novels.   296 pp.; 1925

22. *Native Son*   **Richard Wright**
Bigger Thomas, a black chauffeur, accidentally kills a white girl and then murders his black girlfriend. His relationship with his white lawyer will resonate for today's reader.   359 pp.; 1940

16

MI VIDA LATINA

1. *How the Garcia Girls Lost Their Accents*   **Julia Alvarez**
The displaced daughters of Dr. Garcia belong to the upper-most echelon of Spanish Caribbean society, descendants of the conquistadores, but in this novel they are exiles in the Bronx.   290 pp.; 1991

2. *Bless Me, Ultima*   **Rudolfo Anaya**
This novel by a Mexican-American has sold more than 275,000 copies. It won both the Premio Quinto Sol and the Before Columbus Foundation awards. The old woman, Ultima, is a curandera, a miracle worker who can heal the sick.   248 pp.; 1972

3. *Borderlands/La Frontera:*   **Gloria Anzaldua**
  The New Mestiza
Anzaldua's subject is the devalued identity of Chicano immigrants, and the cultural and sexual identity problems which she says are perpetrated by U.S. racism. The book is a mix of poetry, autobiography, and history. A lesbian feminist, Anzaldua is also the coeditor of *This Bridge Called My Back: Writings by Radical Women of Color.*   203 pp.; 1987

4. *The Perez Family*   **Christine Bell**
Lighthearted novel about Cuban exiles in Miami.
                    256 pp.; 1990

5. *Drink Cultura: Chicanismo*   José Antonio Burciaga
This author describes himself as part Mexicano and part gringo. He offers here twenty-nine lively mini-essays on the Chicano experience, including those about being raised in the basement of an El Paso synagogue where his father was the custodian.   140 pp.; 1993

6. *The Day the Cisco Kid*   Nash Candelaria
   Shot John Wayne
This is a collection of short stories by the author of *Not by the Sword*, winner of an American Book Award. His family helped found Albuquerque, New Mexico, in 1706.
                                                172 pp.; 1988

7. *So Far from God*   Ana Castillo
Riotous novel about the household of Sofi and her four unusual daughters in Tome, New Mexico. In Castillo's *Women Are Not Roses*, lower-class women are in a double bind; they often have to choose between an erotic relationship and class struggle.   252 pp.; 1993

8. *Woman Hollering Creek*   Sandra Cisneros
Winner of the Quality Paperback Club's New Voices Award for 1992, this collection of stories offers tales of women on both sides of the U.S.–Mexico border. It follows *The House on Mango Street*, winner of the 1985 American Book Award from the Before Columbus Foundation.   192 pp.; 1991

9. *Intaglio: A Novel in Six Stories*   Roberta Fernández
Winner of the Multicultural Publishers Exchange Best Book of Fiction, this novel examines the deep-rooted culture of women born at the turn of the century on the U.S–Mexico border.   160 pp.; 1990

10. *The Lonely Crossing of*   J. Joaquin Fraxedas
    Juan Cabrera
Three men escape Castro's Cuba in a flimsy, makeshift raft without realizing that hurricane warnings have been sounded. This novel explicates how spirit and endurance are tested by fate.   174 pp.; 1993

11. *Dreaming in Cuban*   **Cristina Garcia**
Graceful, insightful first novel about three generations of
Cuban women living in Havana, Brooklyn, and near the sea
in Cuba. Watch this writer.   **256 pp.; 1992**

12. *Rainbow's End*   **Genaro Gonzalez**
Gonzalez, the son of migrant workers, is now a professor of
psychology. This first novel was nominated for an American
Book Award.   **200 pp.; 1988**

13. *The Mambo Kings Play*   **Oscar Hijuelos**
    Songs of Love
Pulitzer Prize–winning portrait of a man, his family, and
his community, all in 1950s New York. Even Desi Arnaz
shows up.   **416 pp.; 1989**

14. *Becky and Her Friends*   **Rolando Hinojosa (Smith)**
The most recent installment in the Klail City Death Trip novels, which began in 1972 with the publication of *Estampas
del Valley otras obras*. Hinojosa, whose mother was an Anglo
and whose father was a Mexican-American, is a professor at
the University of Texas.   **160 pp.; 1990**

15. *Zapata Rose in 1992*   **Gary D. Keller**
    & *Other Tales*
Expanded version of *Tales of El Huitlacoche*. Title story
describes the reawakening in 1992 of Emiliano Zapata and
the ways his presence inspires indios, campesinos, and mesti-
zos in the Western Hemisphere.   **326 pp.; 1993**

16. *Latin Moon in Manhattan*   **Jaime Manrique**
For today's Latino immigrants New York City is supposed to
be the promised land. This mystery, whose protagonist is Santiago Martinez, contains a beautiful motorcycle fanatic who
is a lesbian.   **212 pp.; 1992**

17. *Condor and Hummingbird*   **Charlotte Méndez**
                                 (Charlotte Zoë Walker)
The bonds among three women, including an American, as
they build new lives in Bogotá, Colombia.   **137 pp.; 1986**

18. *Nilda*   Nicholasa Mohr
Mohr is a Puerto Rican who lives in Brooklyn. *Nilda* was
selected by the *New York Times* as an Outstanding Book of the
Year. *El Bronx Remembered* was a finalist for the National
Book Award.   292 pp.; 1973

19. *Silent Dancing: A Partial*   Judith Ortiz-Cofer
    Remembrance of a Puerto Rican Childhood
A collection of personal essays by a Puerto Rican–born writer.
Her novel is *The Line of the Sun*.   158 pp.; 1990

20. *Iguana Dreams*   Delia Poey and Virgil Suarez (editors)
Anthology of contemporary fiction that represents the wide
range of cultures and experiences that mark the diverse ethnic
groups of the Latino community.   400 pp.; 1992

21. *Spidertown*   Abraham Rodriguez, Jr.
First novel about a South Bronx ghetto where sixteen-year-
old Miguel, his girlfriend Christalena, his dope dealer boss,
and his roommate, the arsonist, all live on the edge of disaster.   416 pp.; 1993

22. *Days of Obligation: An Argument*   Richard Rodriguez
    with My Mexican Father
Mexico and the United States are portrayed as moral rivals
upon the landscape of California, where Rodriguez lives. In
this book the United States wallows in a culture of tragedy
while Mexico revels in youthful optimism.   230 pp.; 1992

23. *Latinos*   Earl Shorris
A montage of good reporting, oral history, and social analysis
creates a picture of a multifaceted people of varied ancestry—
Mexicans, Puerto Ricans, Cubans, Dominicans, etc.—as they
struggle against both stereotyping and racism and the *racismo*
the groups use against each other.   640 pp.; 1992

24. *Lesser Evils: Ten Quartets*   Gary Soto
A collection of autobiographical essays on writing, women,
childhood, and old age. *Living Up the Street* won the 1985
American Book Award.   142 pp.; 1988

25. *Down These Mean Streets*   **Piri Thomas**
An autobiographical novel, this is one of the best-known works about growing up Puerto Rican in New York City. Thomas lives in California but grew up in El Barrio.

333 pp.; 1967

26. *La Maravilla*   **Alfredo Véa, Jr.**
Here the action is on Buckeye Road in the Arizona of 1958. The novel's symbols are La Maravilla, the blanket of marigolds laid upon graves in Mexican cemeteries, and the mythical dog, sacred to the Aztecs, who returns from the underworld to lead his master to Mictlan, the land of the dead.   **305 pp.; 1993**

27. *The Moths and Other Stories*   **Helena María Viramontes**
Mexican-American Viramontes's stories depict her struggles with her own family and community and against male authority figures. She has quite a bit to say about the Catholic Church too.   **120 pp.; 1985**

17

WAR IS HELL . . . CONTINUED

1. *Dangling Man*   Saul Bellow
A short, intense portrait of a young man waiting to be called
up for military service and caught in the limbo between war
and peace.   **126 pp.; 1944**

2. *Muddy Boots and Red Socks*   Malcolm W. Browne
Along with David Halberstam, with whom he shared a
Pulitzer for coverage of Vietnam, and Neil Sheehan, Browne
is the most reliable reporter on this war. He has seen it all—
from Indochina to the Persian Gulf.   **366 pp.; 1993**

3. *A Good Scent from a*   Robert Olen Butler
   Strange Mountain
Olen's fifteen stories are told from the point of view of a Viet-
namese immigrant to the American Gulf Coast whose sense
of loss stems more from cultural displacement than from the
war. A Pulitzer Prize winner.   **249 pp.; 1993**

4. *Indian Country*   Philip Caputo
Author of *A Rumor of War*, the nonfiction bestseller about
Vietnam, in this novel Caputo writes about a single soldier,
Christian Starkmann, who eleven years after the Vietnam War
still struggles to save his family, his sanity, and his life from
relentless memories of violence.   **432 pp.; 1987**

5. *The Red Badge of Courage*   Stephen Crane

Henry Fleming volunteers to serve with the Union forces, but he is thrown into a panic when he is faced with real fighting. This story is more about the courage of common men than it is about generals, victories, and defeats. A classic not to be missed.   **170 pp.; 1895**

6. *To the White Sea*   James Dickey

A B-29 tailgunner named Muldron is shot down over Tokyo in the last days of World War II. The lone survivor, he strikes out for Hokkaido, the northernmost Japanese island.

275 pp.; 1993

7. *Thai Horse*   William Diehl

Christian Hatcher (also known as the Shadow Warrior) begins to learn the startling secret of Murphy Cody (who was supposedly killed in Vietnam fifteen years ago) and was the son of General William "Buffalo Bill" Cody; he also begins to unravel some secrets in his own past.   **451 pp.; 1988**

8. *Winners and Losers*   Gloria Emerson

An American classic. Emerson traveled across the United States to interview those who fought in Vietnam or opposed that war.   **448 pp.; 1976**

9. *The Best and the Brightest*   David Halberstam

Clearsighted, evenhanded reporting on U.S. politics and government from 1961 to 1969 and the answers to Mailer's question, Why [Were] We in Vietnam?   **688 pp.; 1972**

10. *Paco's Story*   Larry Heinemann

Winner of the National Book Award, this novel reminds readers that the blue-collar men of this country bore the brunt of Vietnam. Like Paco Sullivan, who was in the middle of a firefight and massacre at Fire Base Harriette (a supposedly safe place), these men remain haunted. Read *Close Quarters* too.

210 pp.; 1986

11. *A Farewell to Arms*   Ernest Hemingway

Set on the Italian front during World War II. Frederic Henry, a wounded American ambulance driver, falls in love with his English nurse, Catherine Barkley. If you can get past what you know of Hemingway's sexism and his treatment of women, this is one of his best novels.   332 pp.; 1929

12. *Dispatches* **Michael Herr**
Nonfiction account of the Vietnam years which makes the point that it is hard to arrive at a final truth about this experience.   260 pp.; 1977

13. *A Very Long Engagement* **Sébastien Japrisot**
A French novel about World War I, part romance, part history, part mystery, concerning five French soldiers in January 1917 who try to escape further military service by shooting themselves in the hand. Very worthwhile.   327 pp.; 1993

14. *From Here to Eternity* **James Jones**
Oh, that scene on the beach! One of the great World War II novels, and even the movie is good.   861 pp.; 1951

15. *The Pugilist at Rest* **Thom Jones**
Of the eleven stories in this first book by Jones, those in the first section are about the war in Vietnam and its aftermath in injured lives. Jones was himself discharged from the marines for what was thought to be schizophrenia and later found to be epilepsy.   230 pp.; 1993

16. *Slow Walk in a Sad Rain* **John P. McAfee**
A powerful, darkly comic novel based on the author's experiences as a Green Beret in Vietnam.   256 pp.; 1993

17. *The Naked and the Dead* **Norman Mailer**
Unsurpassed novel about a handful of exhausted men in the Reconnaissance platoon who landed on the beach at Anopopei during World War II. Another set of questions about war was posed in *Why Are We in Vietnam?*

605 pp.; 1951

18. *In Country* **Bobbie Ann Mason**
Bestselling story of a young girl's confrontation with the legacy of Vietnam.   256 pp.; 1985

19. *Chickenhawk*   **Robert Mason**
Gripping Vietnam memoir, concluding with the news that Mason was facing a federal prison sentence for marijuana smuggling. *Chickenhawk: Back in the World* chronicles the author's inability to adjust to civilian life after months of combat duty as a helicopter pilot.   **339 pp.; 1983**

20. *The Green Berets*   **Robin Moore**
Tales of the crack defense teams—paratroopers, frogmen, and commandoes rolled into one—of the Special Forces in Vietnam as they fight a tragic, bewildering war.   **341 pp.; 1965**

21. *Going After Cacciato*   **Tim O'Brien**
Generally considered the best novel about Vietnam. O'Brien's hero walks out of the jungles and begins the 8,600-mile walk to "gay Paree." Don't miss it. *Northern Lights* offers one view of the macho syndrome and its effect on men.

338 pp.; 1978

22. *Machine Dreams*   **Jayne Anne Phillips**
The war in Vietnam splinters the society around the Hampsons of Bellington, West Virginia, and leaves them and the country permanently scarred and changed.   **331 pp.; 1984**

23. *Gardens of Stone*   **Nicholas Proffitt**
This is both a romantic love story and the tale of two men who love the U.S. Army. It is also about the Old Guard, the army's chief ceremonial and burial unit at Arlington National Cemetery—the garden of stone where so many of Vietnam's victims are buried.   **373 pp.; 1983**

24. *Gravity's Rainbow*   **Thomas Pynchon**
This winner of the National Book Award is about Tyrone Slothrop, an American lieutenant stationed in London during World War II. His particular gift is that his erections anticipate German rocket launchings. This is a demanding but extraordinary novel.   **887 pp.; 1973**

25. *All Quiet on the Western Front*   Erich Maria Remarque
The power of this realistic novel of World War I lies in its pas-

sionate hatred of war, experienced in person by the author. After his sudden rise to world fame, he moved to Switzerland in flight from the campaign of hatred and abuse he was subjected to by the right-wing German press. During World War II he wrote *Arch of Triumph* and later *Three Comrades*.

256 pp.; 1929

26. *Arundel*   **Kenneth Roberts**
Arundel, Maine (now called Kennebunkport) is Roberts's ancestral home and that of this novel's main character, Steven Nason—the right-hand man to Benedict Arnold as the Revolutionary War general drives his troops northward toward the walls of Quebec.   **487 pp.; 1956**

27. *Buffalo Afternoon*   **Susan Fromberg Schaeffer**
A novel about three generations of the Bravado family—blue-collar immigrants from Italy to Brooklyn—and what the Vietnam War cost Pete, one of the Bravado sons.   **535 pp.; 1989**

28. *After the War Was Over:*   **Neil Sheehan**
   Hanoi and Saigon
Sheehan won the Pulitzer for *A Bright Shining Lie*. Here he looks at present-day conditions.   **131 pp.; 1992**

29. *Dog Soldiers*   **Robert Stone**
In his second novel, which won the National Book Award for fiction, Stone creates a compelling account of the Vietnam drug trade. In 1971 he was a war correspondent for "a now defunct English imitation of the *Village Voice* called *Ink*." His latest, *Outerbridge Reach*, is a bestseller.   **263 pp.; 1974**

30. *Bad Times, Good Friends*   **Ilse-Margret Vogel**
Actually a memoir, this book traces the attitudes and actions of anti-Nazi Germans and the ways in which Vogel, approaching thirty in the last days of the war, and her friends in Berlin resisted Hitler. Written with complete candor and no attempt to convince the reader of her heroism. **239 pp.; 1992**

18

LOVE IS (ONLY SOMETIMES) A MANY-SPLENDORED THING

1. *Pride and Prejudice*   Jane Austen
Mr. and Mrs. Bennett, five daughters, the irresistible and
autocratic Darcy, lots of love's complications, and multiple
looks at marriage. No one has yet improved on this one, and
they probably can't!   374 pp.; 1813

2. *Sabine's Notebook*   Nick Bantock
Follows *Griffin and Sabine*, with an elusive love affair con-
ducted only by mail. In Volume 1 Sabine is a Solomon
Islander; here she stays in London while Griffin travels and
sends her notes, some of which have to be pulled from
envelopes pasted into the book. A great surprise ending. The
"Extraordinary Correspondence" concludes in *The Golden
Mean*.   unpaged; 1992

3. *Wuthering Heights*   Emily Brontë
Wild Heathcliff and stubborn Catherine, the British moors,
and cruel passion. Published almost 150 years ago but not a
bit outdated!   315 pp.; 1847

4. *Brief Lives*   Anita Brookner
Fay Langdon looks back on her relationships with her hus-

band and lover. Brookner always writes poignantly about the sadness of an unfulfilled life, as in *Hotel du Lac*.

260 pp.; 1991

5. *The Awakening*   Kate Chopin

Rediscovered classic that lay dormant for eighty years, it is the story of the scandal caused by twenty-eight-year-old Edna Pontellier after she discovers passion for the first time in her life.   **341 pp.; 1964**

6. *The Great Gatsby*   F. Scott Fitzgerald

The Jazz Age, bootleggers, and moral failure in the persons of Tom Buchanan, an overaged adolescent, Daisy (who wasn't one), Jordan Baker, a cheat, and Gatsby, a recreated man dominated by dishonesty and obsession. Pay attention to Doctor T. J. Eckleburg when you read this novel, which is one of the greatest written by any American in the twentieth century.   **228 pp.; 1925**

7. *Madame Bovary*   Gustave Flaubert

Emma, the bored wife of a *very* boring French provincial doctor, is shipwrecked before her financial and social ship comes in. Good reasons for this classic to have lasted, and most book clubs read it. Look for multiple images of water.

424 pp.; 1928

8. *Love in the Time of Cholera*   Gabriel García Márquez

This story of unrequited love—fifty years, nine months, and four days worth—is set in a country on the Caribbean coast of South America and ranges from the nineteenth century to the early decades of the twentieth. García Márquez won the Nobel in 1982. And of course, *One Hundred Years of Solitude*.   **348 pp.; 1988**

9. *Whistling and Other Stories*   Myra Goldberg

Tzuris, not hearts and flowers, is what you get in these love stories of New Yorkers battling their way through modern heterosexual encounters, the dating scene, and redefined relationships.   **182 pp.; 1993**

10. *Fear of Flying*   **Erica Jong**
The unforgettable phrase "the zipless fuck" comes (oops!) from this novel. Don't miss it.   **340 pp.; 1973**

11. *Foreign Affairs*   **Alison Lurie**
An American college professor, sensible Vinnie Miner, meets the unsuitable but irresistible Chuck Mumpson on the plane as she goes to London for her sabbatical. Despite his green raincoat and other shortcomings, the inevitable attraction occurs. Winner of a Pulitzer Prize.   **425 pp.; 1984**

12. *I Lock My Door Upon Myself*   **Joyce Carol Oates**
Calla, a mysterious redheaded woman, falls in love with an itinerant water diviner after she has been married off at seventeen to a farmer more than twice her age. The novel was inspired by a painting by the Belgian artist Fernand Khnopff.
       98 pp.; 1990

13. *Mating*   **Norman Rush**
National Book Award–winning novel about an anthropologist in her thirties and a late-forties utopian in 1980s Botswana. His highly praised first book, *Whites*, a story collection, was published in 1986.   **480 pp.; 1991**

14. *Madness of a Seduced*   **Susan Fromberg Schaeffer**
    Woman
Based on a true story. The woman here is driven to murder after she is abandoned by her lover. Good picture of turn-of-the-century Vermont.   **578 pp.; 1983**

15. *After Moondog*   **Jane Shapiro**
First novel about a 1960s marriage initiated when Joanne and William meet while talking to Moondog, the New York street character who wore a Viking helmet and stood on the corner of Fifty-fourth Street and Sixth Avenue for many years. Shapiro has a new and invigorating writing style.
       323 pp.; 1992

16. *The Volcano Lover*   **Susan Sontag**
Story of the eighteenth-century obsessive collector, Sir William

Hamilton, a cuckold to remember, his seductive wife, Emma, and her lover, Admiral Nelson—with plenty of hypocrisy about women and privilege on the side.   **419 pp.; 1992**

17. *Anna Karenina*   **Leo Tolstoy**
The archetypal story of the conflict between maternal and sexual love, in nineteenth-century Russia and everywhere else, and never surpassed in the telling by any writer.

855 pp.; 1900

18. *The Accidental Tourist*   **Anne Tyler**
Muriel Pritchett, an inventive survivor, falls into the life of Macon Leary, and Muriel's eccentric, disorderly world becomes Macon's gentle reprieve.   **355 pp.; 1985**

19. *A Handful of Dust*   **Evelyn Waugh**
Satire of a certain stratum of English life where all the characters have money—but not much else. A marriage breaks up here from the wife's terminal boredom; the parasite she chooses next is worse than the husband.   **308 pp.; 1932**

20. *Ethan Frome*   **Edith Wharton**
Watch out for trees if you're on that final sleigh ride with the niece of your boring, angry wife; even unconsummated love affairs can be very dangerous! This is, simply, a great, almost existential book about wasted lives.   **260 pp.; 1911**

21. *Written on the Body*   **Jeanette Winterson**
Fourth novel from this British writer, this one describing an erotic affair between the narrator, whose gender we do not know, and Louise, unhappily married to a workaholic cancer researcher.   **192 pp.; 1992**

19

FROM ASIAN SHORES

1. *A Planet of Eccentrics*   Ven Begamudré
Short stories by a Saskatchewan writer of East Indian heritage, these tales tell of lost roots and cultural isolation.

196 pp.; 1990

2. *Donald Duk*   Frank Chin
The main character is a twelve-year-old kid, confused about his ethnic heritage, with a name he most certainly doesn't like! Chin's story collection, *The Chinaman Pacific & Frisco R.R. Co.*, won the American Book Award. He is also a playwright.   **173 pp.; 1991**

3. *Clear Light of Day*   Anita Desai
Nominated for the Booker, this novel and *Fire on the Mountain*, winner of India's National Academy of Letters Award, both depict the struggle that middle-class Indian women face in harmonizing societal demands and their own needs.

192 pp.; 1980

4. *Charlie Chan is Dead*   Jessica Hagedorn (editor)
An anthology of contemporary Asian-American fiction including stories by Gish Jen, Amy Tan, and Maxine Hong Kingston.   **640 pp.; 1992**

5. *Typical American*   Gish Jen
Charming, powerful look at the Chang family as they come
to New York for education and safety, and find money
hunger and fried chicken franchises. A writer to watch.

                                              296 pp.; 1991

6. *The Floating World*   Cynthia Kadohata
In a unique coming-of-age story, a Japanese-American adolescent goes on the road with Obasan, her grandmother, the rest
of the family, and visits her father, a chicken sexer in
Arkansas.   **196 pp.; 1989**

7. *Paint the Yellow Tiger*   Dong Kingman
Memoirs of life in China, Hong Kong, and the United States
by the Chinese-American artist. Includes many of his water-
colors and information about technique, composition, and
color.   **128 pp.; 1991**

8. *Tripmaster Monkey*   Maxine Hong Kingston
In her first work of fiction, Kingston creates Wittman Ah
Sing, a word-drunk Chinese-American one year out of Berke-
ley, who dreams of writing a huge work encompassing novels
and folktales, finding his grandmother, and living when the
Beats ruled San Francisco.   **340 pp.; 1989**

9. *Obasan*   Joy Kogawa
Kogawa, a Canadian of Japanese ancestry, writes here of the
internment of the Japanese in Canada during World War II.
Obasan won both the Books in Canada First Novel Award
and the Canadian Authors' Association Book of the Year
Award.   **250 pp.; 1982**

10. *China Boy*   Gus Lee
Funny coming-of-age novel in 1950s San Francisco and a very
different vision of America by a writer who attended West
Point and received a law degree from the University of California. His real name is Augustus Samuel Mein-Sun Lee.

                                              322 pp.; 1991

11. *The Disappearing Moon Cafe*   Skye Lee

In 1986 Kae Ying Woo searches for the "bones," or memories, of her ancestors as her great-grandfather, Wong Gwei Chang, walked the tracks of the Canadian Pacific Railway in British Columbia in 1892, looking for the actual bones of his dead countrymen.   237 pp.; 1991

12. *The Forbidden Stitch*   Shirley Geok-Lim,
                                                  Mayumi Tsutakawa,
                                          Margarita Donnely (editors)

This is an "Asian American Women's Anthology" including more than eighty contributors, many of them new voices. Winner of the 1990 American Book Award.   290 pp.; 1989

13. *Pangs of Love*   David Wong Louie

Inventive first collection of short stories filled with puzzled protagonists and particularly good on the spaces between generations in the Chinese-American Pang family.

                                                          225 pp.; 1991

14. *Talking to High Monks in the Snow*   Lydia Minatoya

This memoir, subtitled *An Asian American Odyssey*, is about growing up as a Japanese-American in the Albany of the 1950s, the relocation of the author's parents during World War II, and her subsequent visit to Japan in the 1980s to reconcile the problems of actuality and inheritance.

                                                          288 pp.; 1992

15. *Sour Sweet*   Timothy Mo

This novel about a Chinese man, Chen, living in one of London's seedier neighborhoods, was shortlisted for the Booker. He must deal both with his ambitious wife and with the troubling demands of the Hung family, a traditional Triad society that governs life in his community. Mo is one of Britain's hottest writers.   278 pp.; 1985

16. *The Middleman and Other Stories*   Bharati Mukherjee

A winner of the National Book Critics Circle award, this collection concentrates on human failings in those displaced from the East and in the home-grown product as well.

206 pp.; 1988

17. *Bone*   Fae Myenne Ng

Ng takes readers into the hidden heart of San Francisco's Chinatown to a world of the Leong family's secrets, hidden shame and the lost bones of a "paper father." The relationship between sisters is interesting here. Watch this author.

194 pp.; 1993

18. *The Joy Luck Club*   Amy Tan

In 1949 four Chinese women begin meeting in San Francisco to play mah jongg, invest in stocks, eat dim sum, and "say" stories. If you change the names, this is in many ways the story of all immigrants and the generation that succeeds them. Astounding debut novel that transcends ethnicity, place, and time.   288 pp.; 1989

19. *Talking to the Dead*   Sylvia Watanabe

Beautifully linked stories of an ancient and modern world and a journey through the minefields of adolescence, betrayal, madness, racism, and disillusion by a Japanese-American from Hawaii. Don't miss it.   127 pp.; 1992

20. *Homebase*   Shawn Wong

Four generations of one Chinese-American family have their roots in a laborer who arrived in northern California in the nineteenth century to find the illusionary paradise, Gum Sahn, or Gold Mountain. Rainsford Chan tells their story.

98 pp.; 1991

21. *In Desert Run: Poems and Stories*   Mitsuye Yamada

The setting for the title story is the camp in Idaho where Yamada's family was interned during World War II; it describes the emotional landscape of a woman who has never felt completely safe since then. Yamada was born in Japan and grew up in Seattle.   112 pp.; 1988

22. *Seventeen Syllables*   **Hisaye Yamamoto**

Yamamoto is the winner of the 1986 American Book Award for Lifetime Achievement from the Before Columbus Foundation. Several of the stories are concerned with her mother's experience in the relocation camps for Japanese-Americans during World War II and the problems of the Nisei and Issei in the United States.   **134 pp.; 1988**

20

ONE TO BEAM UP, MR. SCOTT

Science Fiction by Men

1. *Helliconia Summer*   **Brian W. Aldiss**
This is the second book in a trilogy about the planet of Helliconia, where one year lasts two and a half thousand years and winter is seven centuries long. *Helliconia Winter* and *Helliconia Spring* are also recommended.   **398 pp.; 1984**

2. *The Foundation Trilogy*   **Isaac Asimov**
Foundation is the colony founded by Hari Seldon and his band of Encyclopedists. This Hugo Award–winning trilogy—*Foundation*, *Foundation and Empire*, and *Second Foundation*—covers nearly four centuries of the rise of civilization from barbarism. Asimov wrote 260 books before his death in 1993.   **225 pp.; 1951**

3. *The Drowned World*   **J. G. Ballard**
Written by the idiosyncratic author of the autobiographical novel of wartime Shanghai, *Empire of the Sun*. His is a world of disaster, an interplay between man and the environment, written in a very polished style.   **316 pp.; 1962**

4. *The Demolished Man*   Alfred Bester

Lincoln Powell is a telepathic cop in A.D. 2301 where the police stop murder before it happens. But not this time. The D.A., by the way, is a crusty but fair-minded computer. Won the first-ever Hugo Award of 1953.   183 pp.; 1953

5. *A Case of Conscience*   James Blish

Blish builds the stories of four extraordinary men in two separate and complete worlds, idyllic Lithia and a culture on earth that has gone below ground into a world of subcities. Also *The Stars My Destination*.   188 pp.; 1958

6. *The Martian Chronicles*   Ray Bradbury

Considered the masterpiece of his twenty-four books, this is about the men of Earth who arrived on Mars in glittering rockets to find masked men who spoke their minds. Also *Fahrenheit 451*, about fascism and bookburning; great but not science fiction.   204 pp.; 1954

7. *Stand on Zanzibar*   John Brunner

First published twenty-five years ago, this novel takes place in 2010 when seven-billion-plus earthlings live in an age of acceleratubes and Moonbase Zero. It features a riot-torn New York City, an Asian island threatened by a volcano, and the plague-ridden African Beninia. The future in Brunner's novels is dark, overpopulated, and polluted.   505 pp.; 1968

8. *Lost Boys*   Orson Scott Card

Enlarged version of Card's autobiographical short story by the same name. The Fletchers, devout Mormons, have a depressed son, Stevie, who has imaginary friends. Their problems start when real boys with the names of those friends start disappearing. Card wrote *The Memory of Earth*, *Xenocide*, and *Songbird*.   447 pp.; 1992

9. *Childhood's End*   Arthur C. Clarke

Clarke has written thirty books which together have sold two million copies in fifteen languages. This classic is the story of the last generation of humankind on earth. He wrote *A Space*

Odyssey, from which came the film *2001*, and won the 1979 Nebula Award for *The Fountains of Paradise*.

216 pp.; 1953

10. *Mission of Gravity*   **Hal Clement**
This novel reveals the demands of the Mesklinites and one of their sea captains (named Barlennan) when they recover a rocket for the earthmen. One of the best hard science writers.

224 pp.; 1953

11. *The Einstein Intersection*   **Samuel R. Delany**
This won the Nebula. Delany writes what are known as space operas. He has won the Hugo and Nebula awards for his speculative novels, where psychology, mythology, and imagery play a big part.   **155 pp.; 1967**

12. *The Man in the High Castle*   **Philip K. Dick**
A fine alternative world novel in which Dick's typically complex, believable (and often schizophrenic) characters are on display. Because of the movie *Blade Runner*—made from his novel *Do Androids Dream of Electric Sleep?*—he is now a cult figure.   **239 pp.; 1962**

13. *Deathbird Stories*   **Harlan Ellison**
Here are nineteen stories, fantasies, and allegories written over a period of ten years, including "Pretty Maggie Money Eyes" and "The Whimper of Whipped Dogs." Ellison has won five Hugo awards.   **334 pp.; 1975**

14. *Alas, Babylon!*   **Pat Frank**
This is a novel about the end of the world (courtesy of an H-bomb attack) and the day after that. How would you survive on a planet poisoned with radiation?   **279 pp.; 1959**

15. *Neuromancer*   **William Gibson**
This postmodern work won the Hugo, Nebula, and Philip K. Dick awards. Case was the best interface who ever ran in Earth's computer matrix, but he got caught in a double cross! Also *Count Zero* and *Burning Chrome*. He wrote *The Difference Engine* with Bruce Sterling.   **271 pp.; 1984**

16. *The Forever War*   Joe Haldeman

Haldeman's experience in Vietnam and his scientific training are obvious in his hard science fiction novels. He wrote *Worlds*, *Worlds Apart*, and won the Nebula for this one.

236 pp.; 1975

17. *The Moon Is a Harsh Mistress*   Robert A. Heinlein

Heinlein is an authorial descendant of Chandler and Hammett. His novels are often funny (even sentimental) and unusually bright compared to the traditional dark vision. He is a major writer in this genre. Also *Beyond This Horizon*, *Double Star*, and especially *Stranger in a Strange Land*.

383 pp.; 1966

18. *Good News from Outerspace*   John Kessel

Much admired for this novel, Kessel won the 1982 Nebula for best novella for *Another Orphan*. "Buffalo" describes an encounter between Kessel's immigrant father and his idol, H. G. Wells.   **402 pp.; 1989**

19. *A Canticle for Leibowitz*   Walter M. Miller, Jr.

After winning a Hugo in 1961, Miller—like Leibowitz, a convert to Catholicism—has largely been silent. The story takes place in a monastery in the American Southwest after a nuclear war and was perhaps influenced by the American bombing of the Monte Cassino monastery in Italy during World War II.   **320 pp.; 1959**

20. *Red Mars*   Kim Stanley Robinson

In Robinson a more humanistic, literary, and softer science fiction is on display. *The Wild Shore* and *Pacific Edge* are by him too.   **519 pp.; 1993**

21. *Dying Inside*   Robert Silverberg

Silverberg started as a writer of pulp novels but is now greatly respected as an accomplished artist in this genre. As the *New York Times* said, *Kingdoms of the Wall* "is a parable about the danger of seeking more intimate contact with the powers that control the universe." *A Time of Changes* won the Nebula in 1971.   **245 pp.; 1972**

22. *Way Station*   Clifford Simak
Now thirty years old, this story of the solitary Enoch Wallace, who manages the Way Station and is earth's sole representative to the Inter-Galactic Council, still holds up wonderfully. Simak won the International Fantasy Award for *City*; as with Bradbury, his midwestern roots are obvious.   **210 pp.; 1963**

23. *Bug Jack Barron*   Norman Spinrad
An unusual novel in this genre because it is really about television, power, business, and more power. His latest is *Deux X*, in which he wonders when a computer replica of a personality becomes the equivalent of a living person. *Stations of the Tide* is about a functionary caught between a humdrum bureaucracy and what James Morrow calls "the alluring Ur-reality fashioned by the protean wizard Gregorian."
                                                         327 pp.; 1969

24. *More Than Human*   Theodore Sturgeon
Five extraordinary individuals "blesh" in this one, thereby losing their separate identities. Unfortunately, only one of them is aware that some very important part of this new Self is missing.   **186 pp.; 1953**

25. *War of the Worlds*   H. G. Wells
Many of science fiction's most familiar concepts—the time machine and the invading alien—emerged in this actual radio broadcast heard on "Mercury Theatre On the Air." Most listeners thought the events were real, not fictional. Also, of course, *The Time Machine*.   **149 pp.; 1938**

26. *The Book of the New Sun, 4 vols.*   George Wolfe
Wolfe combines science fiction and fantasy, and often complex, subtle writing is on display here. *The Citadel of the Autarch* (317 pp.), *The Claw of the Conciliator* (303 pp.), *The Shadow of the Torturer* (303 pp.), and *The Sword of the Lictor* (302 pp.).   *Citadel*, **1983**; *Claw*, **1981**;
                                       Shadow, **1980**; *Sword*, **1981**

Science Fiction by Women

1. *The Darkover Novels*   **Marian Zimmer Bradley**
This is a trilogy composed of *Landfall* (1972), *Sword of Chaos,* and *Leroni of Darkover* (1991) by the extremely popular writer of science fiction.

Sword of Chaos: **240 pp.; 1982**

2. *Xenogenesis* (trilogy)   **Octavia E. Butler**
All of Butler's novels feature black women struggling against racism and sexism: *Kindred, Patternmaster, Mind of My Mind,* and *Wild Seed. Bloodchild* won the Nebula for best novelette in 1984.   **726 pp.; 1987–89**

3. *Synners*   **Pat Cadigan**
Nominated for the 1991 Nebula. Her women, like those males in the usual cyberpunk, are the center of a high-tech, low-life adventure story.   **435 pp.; 1991**

4. *Walk to the End of the World*   **Suzy McKee Charnas**
Like Tepper, Charnas tries to dissuade the reader from accepting the obligation of men to act as macho maniacs after a nuclear world war. *The Unicorn Tapestry* won the 1980 Nebula for best novella.   **214 pp.; 1974**

5. *Hellburner*   **S. J. Cherryh**
Cherryh writes good space romps. *The Faded Sun: Kesrith; The Faded Sun: Shon 'Jir;* and *The Faded Sun: Kulath* provide an extended study of an alien race. In her novels women are in positions of absolute power.   **432 pp.; 1981**

6. *Artificial Things*   **Karen Joy Fowler**
Collection of fine short stories by the author of *Sarah Canary*.   **218 pp.; 1986**

7. *Carpathians*   **Janet Frame**
As the *New York Times* noted, "the inhabitants of a New Zealand town must come to grips with a frightening new reality: the gravitational effects of a quasar have distorted all perception of time and space."   **196 pp.; 1988**

8. *Herland*   **Charlotte Perkins Gilman**
An early twentieth-century story, included here for historical interest, that describes a land without men. If you read her novella *The Yellow Wallpaper*, you'll understand why Gilman wrote this one. *Herland* was written in 1915 and serialized in Gilman's monthly magazine, *The Forerunner*.

147 pp.; 1979 (reprint)

9. *Dream Years*   **Lisa Goldstein**
Bizarre characters and fable: a good mix. Also *The Red Magician*.   181 pp.; 1985

10. *Beggars in Spain*   **Nancy Kress**
Her novella with the same title won the 1991 Nebula. This is a brave new world of genetically engineered prodigies who are so smart they don't have to sleep. A good look at new hierarchies and corruption among an elite. Also *Brain Rose*.

448 pp.; 1993

11. *The Left Hand of Darkness*   **Ursula K. Le Guin**
A Nebula winner, this is on everyone's list and promotes great discussions. LeGuin creates Winter, a backward world, where all humans are the same sex. Also *Planet of Exile*, *The Dispossessed*, and *City of Illusions*.   286 pp.; 1969

12. *Dreamsnake*   **Vonda N. McIntyre**
The plots are complex and tightly written here, perhaps because of her work in movies. She has a humanistic side that is refreshing in this genre.   313 pp.; 1978

13. *Daughters of Earth*   **Judith Merril**
Three novelettes: *Project Nursemaid*, *Daughters of Earth*, and *Homecalling*. The first two involve women's sacrifices and obstacles in space exploration, and the third is about two children stranded on a strange planet.   255 pp.; 1969

14. *The Ragged World*   **Judith Moffett**
Furry aliens, time travel, and cosmic events reign here.

341 pp.; 1991

15. *Doorway into Time*   C. L. Moore
Really a tale first published in a September issue of *Famous
Fantastic Mysteries*. Cloaked in the alias of Lawrence O'Don-
nell, she was hailed then as an extraordinary discovery—a
writer of the supernatural and the horrifying—and published
by *Weird Tales* magazine. Now she is the most outstanding
woman writing in this field.   **1943**

16. *The Falling Woman*   Pat Murphy
Won the 1987 Nebula for Best Novel. Also *Rachel in Love*.
                                              287 pp.; 1986

17. *Woman on the Edge of Time*   Marge Piercy
Consuelo Ramos, a Chicana in New York, is the woman in
question, and through her we see how one person, perceived
as faceless and invisible, becomes a potential subject for a
neuro-electric experiment. Her future is in Mattapoisett, a
playful, androgynous society. Piercy wrote *Small Changes*,
many books of poetry, and *Gone to Soldiers*.   **369 pp.; 1976**

18. *The Female Man*   Joanna Russ
This is a novel about polarities—the individual and society,
the actual and the possible, women and men—by one of the
very best writers in this genre. Find a copy of her 1972 short
story, "When It Changed."   **287 pp.; 1975**

19. *Venus of Shadows*   Pamela Sargent
In *Venus of Dreams* Iris Angharads works on the Venus Project, an effort to carve a green and growing world out of the
hellish wilderness of that planet. A generation later her children must find their way in that world. Sargent is famous for
The Shore of Omen.   **544 pp.; 1988**

20. *Mess-Mend: The Yankees*   Marietta Shaginian
     in Petrograd
Written by a Muscovite under the pseudonym Jim Dollar, this
was published in biweekly installments in the Soviet Union
seventy years ago. The hero is named Thingmaster.
                                              375 pp.; 1923

21. *The Gate to Women's Country*   **Sheri Tepper**
In the walled towns of Women's Country, women and nonviolent men nurture what is left of the past after the world all but burned to ash 300 years ago in the flames of a nuclear holocaust. Stavia and Chernon have to cope with it all. Tepper wrote *After Long Silence* and *The Awakeners*.

278 pp.; 1988

22. *Brightness Falls from the Air*   **James Tiptree, Jr.**
Born Alice Sheldon, the author had the last laugh when male critics claimed that her sharp, pointed novels could only have been written by a man.   **382 pp.; 1985**

23. *The Snow Queen*   **Joan Vinge**
A Hugo winner featuring complex characters and mythic resonances. *The Summer Queen* is its sequel.   **536 pp.; 1980**

24. *And the Angels Sing*   **Kate Wilhelm**
A dozen short stories, including "The Look Alike," in which a grieving young mother meets a doppelganger of her lost daughter.   **320 pp.; 1992**

25. *The Doomsday Book*   **Connie Willis**
Winner of multiple Nebula and Hugo awards and much praise for her first novel, *Lincoln's Dreams*, Willis writes here about Kiurin, who gets trapped in the Middle Ages when past and future become strangely linked.   **445 pp.; 1992**

GAY WRITES

1. *Trash*   **Dorothy Allison**
A collection of short stories by the now-famed author of *Bastard Out of Carolina*.   **174 pp.; 1988**

2. *Nightwood*   **Djuna Barnes**
A novel about a lesbian love affair by the well-known writer who was a central figure in the literary community in Paris during the 1920s.   **211 pp.; 1946**

3. *The Body and Its Dangers*   **Allen Barnett**
Short stories about where desire leads, with some poignant insights about the devastation of AIDS and the everyday loneliness of most people.   **181 pp.; 1990**

4. *Coming Out Under Fire*   **Allan Berube**
Ten years in the writing, this is a vivid portrait of the life and times of gay men and women during World War II. They fought two wars: one for their country, another for their own survival.   **287 pp.; 1990**

5. *Gentlemen, I Address You Privately*   **Kay Boyle**
Originally published sixty years ago and revised in 1990. Munday, an English priest defrocked for playing "Poeme de l'Extase" during collection, exiles himself to Normandy.

There he becomes sexually involved with Ayton, a Cockney sailor. Included here for historical value and an early look at homosexuality.   **227 pp.; 1933**

6. *Rubyfruit Jungle*   **Rita Mae Brown**
Like her heroine in this novel, Brown was an orphan born out of wedlock. *High Hearts*, the latest book by this former lesbian separatist, is about southern women who, disguised as men, fought in the Civil War.   **217 pp.; 1973**

7. *A Home at the End of the World*   Michael Cunningham
Jonathan Glover and Bobby Morrow, childhood friends from Cleveland, and Clare, a veteran of New York's erotic wars, try to create a new kind of family in New York City and upstate.   **343 pp.; 1990**

8. *White on Black on White*   **Coleman Dowell**
A neglected but excellent writer from the generation of Tennessee Williams, James Purdy, Gore Vidal, et al. This book is about race, relationships, and homosexuality. His memoir is *A Star Bright Lie*.   **251 pp.; 1983**

9. *Odd Girls and Twilight Lovers*   **Lillian Faderman**
A lesbian feminist, Faderman is Distinguished Professor of English at California State University in Fresno. She wrote *Surpassing the Love of Men*, a history of romantic friendship, and *Scotch Verdict*, about two nineteenth-century Victorian lesbians who were brought to trial. This is the definitive study of lesbian life in America from the turn of the century to today.   **373 pp.; 1991**

10. *Murder at the Nightwood Bar*   Katherine V. Forrest
Forrest writes the Kate Delafield mysteries, and in this one, the Los Angeles police detective, a midforties lesbian, solves a case of child abuse. Also *Curious Wine*.   **220 pp.; 1987**

11. *Annie on My Mind*   **Nancy Garden**
Because of a disaster at school, Liza puts aside her feelings for Annie. Eventually love triumphs over ignorance.
                                                   233 pp.; 1982

12. *What the Dead Remember*   **Harlan Greene**
An exquisitely told southern novel about a young boy growing up in Charleston, South Carolina, and his coming of age
there as an adult. Also read *We Never Danced the
Charleston*.   **180 pp.; 1991**

13. *The Well of Loneliness*   **Radclyffe Hall**
Largely autobiographical; this is Hall's attempt to deal with
lesbian identity in novel form. She was prosecuted for obscen-
ity, and the novel was suppressed.   **506 pp.; 1928**

14. *Country of Old Men: The Last*   **Joseph Hansen**
     Dave Brandstetter Mystery
Hansen created the gay detective story with a series of twelve
mysteries featuring gay insurance investigator Dave Brand-
stetter. This one received the 1992 Lambda Literary Award.
                                                     248 pp.; 1991

15. *Dancer from the Dance*   **Andrew Holleran**
This is the classic disco era "gay novel," which more or less
defined the genre.   **250 pp.; 1978**

16. *Let the Dead Bury Their Dead*   **Randall Kenan**
Kenan creates Horace Cross, a member of the oldest and
proudest black family in Tims Creek, North Carolina, four
generations of whom are caught in tradition and transformation. An exciting new voice.   **257 pp.; 1993**

17. *The Normal Heart*   **Larry Kramer**
Kramer is a longtime activist and probably the most vocifer-
ous speaker on AIDS and the failure of America to treat it in
time. This book includes an introduction by the novelist
Andrew Holleran and a foreword by the late Joseph Papp.
                                                     123 pp.; 1985

18. *Angels in America*   **Tony Kushner**
Subtitled *A Gay Fantasia on National Themes*, this award-
winning, well-received Broadway play has two parts. Part
One is *Millennium Approaches*. Part Two is *Perestroika*.
Don't miss it.   **90 pp.; 1993**

19. *The Lost Language of Cranes*   David Leavitt
Following *Family Dancing* and *Equal Affections*, Leavitt writes here of the troubled marriage of Rose and Owen Benjamin. She longs for more passion in her life; he secretly watches pornographic movies on Sunday afternoons; and their son, Philip, is in the midst of a gay affair. **319 pp.; 1986**

20. *Zani: A New Spelling of My Name*   Audre Lorde
A self-described "radical, Black, lesbian, feminist," Lorde died recently. This is her autobiography, which she called a "biomythography." She is best known as a poet, as in *Undersong: Chosen Poems*.   **256 pp.; 1982**

21. *Object of My Affection*   Stephan McCauley
In this one George Mullen is gay, Nina Borowski is straight *and* pregnant; they're best friends and roommates; a kooky, sweet, unusual tale of New York life. Followed by *The Easy Way Out*.   **316 pp.; 1987**

22. *Making History*   Eric Marcus
A series of absorbing first-person accounts of fifty men and women and their long struggle for gay rights. **532 pp.; 1992**

23. *Tales of the City*   Armistead Maupin
Portrait of the agonies and absurdities of modern urban life in San Francisco in one volume of a series of Maupin tales.
271 pp.; 1978

24. *Conduct Unbecoming*   Randy Shilts
Epic-length book based on more than 1,100 interviews, it traces the history of discrimination against gays in the military, dating back to the Revolution.   **784 pp.; 1993**

25. The *City and the Pillar*   Gore Vidal
Vidal, who assiduously rejected modernism and the modern novel, wrote one of the first books to touch on homosexual themes. *Myra Breckinridge* is considered to be a transsexual novel.   **249 pp.; 1948**

26. *The Front Runner*   Patricia Nell Warren
Considered a gay *Catcher in the Rye*, this is the story of Billy

Conners, who realizes at sixteen that he's a little different, a little "weird." Not as violent as many novels with homosexual themes and quite touching.   346 pp.; 1974

27. *Genet, A Biography*   **Edmund White**
This biography of Jean Genet, one of France's most original and forceful novelists and playwrights (who was also a thief and a pederast), places Genet's personal and literary vision squarely in his exclusively homosexual experience. White is the author of *A Boy's Life*, which deals with his own homosexuality.   **728 pp.; 1993**

28. *Oranges Are Not the Only Fruit*   **Jeanette Winterson**
Semiautobiographical first novel, a coming-out story of a young British girl in the 1960s who is adopted into an evangelical household in the dour industrial midlands.

177 pp.; 1987

29. *The Safe Sea of Women*   **Bonnie Zimmerman (editor)**
Collection of lesbian fiction from 1969 to 1989 that should be read as part of the history of American writing women.

273 pp.; 1990

22

IN CARIBBEAN WATERS

1. *Bake Face and Other Guava Stories*   Opal Palmer Adisa
The newest book by this Jamaican poet is *Travelling Women*.
116 pp.; 1986

2. *Sans Souci*   **Dionne Brand**
Brand is a Canadian poet and activist born in Trinidad. Her work portrays the themes of alienation, domination, racism, and sexism in her own life and in the societies of Canada and the Caribbean.   **150 pp.; 1989**

3. *No Telephone to Heaven*   **Michelle Cliff**
This lyrical novel by the Jamaican-American writer tells Clare Savage's story as she searches for self and place. The island itself is a character in this beautiful book. Her new novel is *Free Enterprise*.   **211 pp.; 1987**

4. *I, Tituba, Black Witch of Salem*   **Maryse Condé**
Written in French, this postmodern novel won the 1986 Grand Prix Litteraire de la Femme. It expands on the true story of the West Indian slave Tituba, who was accused of witchcraft in Salem, Massachusetts, arrested in 1692, and forgotten in jail until the general amnesty for witches two years later. A wonderful but violent read.   **240 pp.; 1992**

5. *Beka Lamb*   **Zee Edgell**

This novel, which won the Fawcett Society Book Prize in 1982, focuses on the coming to consciousness of a young girl and her understanding of how Belize society functions.

172 pp.; 1986

6. *Green Cane and Juicy Flotsam*   **Carmen C. Esteves and Lizabeth Paravisini-Gebert (editors)**

A new collection of work by Caribbean writers and a fine way to get to know more about this part of the world.

273 pp.; 1991

7. *The Guyana Quartet*   **Wilson Harris**

Contains *Palace of the Peacock*, *The Far Journey of Oudin*, *The Whole Armour*, and *The Secret Ladder*, all by this Guyanan writer.   **464 pp.; 1985**

8. *Crick Crack Monkey*   **Merle Hodge**

The heroine, Tess, grows up amid the class and cultural confusions in Trinidad in the midtwentieth century. This is a good look at the sociopolitical realities on this island.

112 pp.; 1981

9. *Lucy*   **Jamaica Kincaid**

A teenage girl from the West Indies comes to North America to work as an au pair for Lewis and Mariah and their four children. At the same time she unravels the mysteries of her own sexuality. *Annie John* tells the first half of the story.

164 pp.; 1990

10. *Harriet's Daughter*   **Marlene Noubese Philip**

This story centers on the friendship between two girls: Margaret, a second-generation Canadian whose father is from Barbados and whose mother is Jamaican, and Zulma, who arrives from Tobago to live with her mother and stepfather. Philip is a Canadian.   **150 pp.; 1988**

11. *Cambridge*   **Caryl Phillips**

A novel set in the nineteenth century that tells two stories:

one, about an English plantation owner's daughter and another, about Cambridge, a proud and powerful slave.

192 pp.; 1992

12. *Wide Sargasso Sea*   Jean Rhys
Born into the minority white community of Dominica, Rhys focused on the conflict Creoles faced in the Caribbean and in England. A great favorite of reading clubs, this novel tells the story of Antoinette Cosway, who ends up supposedly "mad" in the attic of an English house. Sound familiar?

189 pp.; 1967

13. *Summer Lightning*   Olive Senior
First collection of short stories by a Jamaican novelist, poet, and dramatist that won the Commonwealth Writers Prize in 1987. As with many writers from the Caribbean, her subject is often childhood.   **134 pp.; 1986**

14. *The Bridge of Beyond*   Simone Schwarz-Bart
A native of Guadaloupe in the French Antilles, she takes a Creole world view of magic and the strength of family. She wrote, with her Jewish husband Andre Schwarz-Bart, *A Dish of Pork with Green Bananas*.   **246 pp.; 1974**

15. *Easy in the Islands*   Bob Shacochis
This first novel won the American Book Award. It is set on an imaginary island in the Lesser Antilles where the hero celebrates the reappearance of his first love, the volatile Johanna.

480 pp.; 1993

16. *The Hills of Hebron*   Sylvia Wynter
Wynter was born in Cuba of Jamaican parents. Her only novel deals with madness, race, class, and the psyche of a physically handicapped person.   **315 pp.; 1962**

23

LA, LA, LA, IT'S MAGIC

1. *The House of the Spirits*   **Isabel Allende**
Chilean novelist's saga of Esteban Trueba's family. Allende
contrasts Trueba's patriarchal attitude to the imaginative spiritual life of his wife, Clara, and spotlights the violence done
to women. The model for Clara was Allende's own mother.
The Tales of Eva Luna is a book of short stories.

                                                        368 pp.; 1985

2. *Labyrinths*   **Jorge Luís Borges**
A metaphysical Argentinian writer whose short stories are
intellectually (as opposed to emotionally) driven. This work is
a good introduction to why he was so influential before his
death in 1986.   243 pp.; 1962

3. *Illywhacker*   **Peter Carey**
Imagination is everything, so this extraordinary surreal tale is
written by a 139-year-old man. *Bliss* is hell, so to speak.

                                                        600 pp.; 1985

4. *Wise Children*   **Angela Carter**
Her eleventh and final novel, this is a mock memoir that is
narrated by an endlessly imaginative postmodernist old
woman, and tells the story of unusual illegitimate twin
daughters.   234 pp.; 1992

5. *Taratuta/Still Life with Pipe*   José Donoso

Two novellas about a young man's obsession with a now-forgotten painter and the ways in which fiction and history intertwine. Read *The Garden Next Door* too.   160 pp.; 1993

6. *The Beet Queen*   Louise Erdrich

Spans forty years, beginning when a brother and sister, abandoned by their peculiar mother, arrive by boxcar in Argus, a small off-reservation town in North Dakota, to live with their Aunt Fritzie, and her husband, Pete. This is a novel about miracles, the magic of natural events, and the mystery in the human condition.   338 pp.; 1986

7. *The Old Gringo*   Carlos Fuentes

Ambrose Bierce, the American writer, soldier, and journalist, spends his last mysterious days in Mexico among Pancho Villa's men. His encounter with Tomas Arroyo, one of Villa's generals, is symbolic of the conflict between these two cultures. Many readers believe that *The Death of Artemio Cruz* is Fuentes's best novel.   199 pp.; 1985

8. *The General in His Labyrinth*   Gabriel García Márquez

This novel transmutes historical truth about Simón Bolívar, the liberator who tried to free South America from Spanish domination, into magical narrative.   285 pp.; 1990

9. *Winter's Tale*   Mark Helprin

In the year 2000 New York becomes the golden city people have always desired, complete with a milkhouse that can fly, a manic billionaire who commutes to East Hampton by blimp, and a love affair between a second-story man and Beverly Penn, the daughter of the mansion.   673 pp.; 1983

10. *Dune*   Frank Herbert

Herbert is interested in the tensions between humanity and the environment. The sequence of *Dune* books form a serious space opera, complete with Galactic empires, storm troopers, etc.   412 pp.; 1965

11. *Aunt Julia and the Scriptwriter*　　Maria V. Llosa
A comic, ribald, sophisticated tale of life and love in Lima in
the 1950s. In other words, Mario falls in love with his thirty-
two-year-old aunt.　　**374 pp.; 1982**

12. *Maqroll*　　Alvaro Mutis
Three novellas featuring Maqroll the Gaviero (the Lookout),
an adventurer whose dubious schemes include smuggling,
managing a brothel, and an unwitting involvement with
South American guerrillas.　　**288 pp.; 1992**

13. *The Famished Road*　　Ben Okri
Okri presents a crowded, impoverished African village where
visitors arrive from the spirit world. Winner of the Booker
Prize.　　**500 pp.; 1992**

14. *Sunstone*　　Octavio Paz
One of the great modern long poems by Mexico's leading
poet. Get the edition with the translation by Muriel Rukeyser.
　　59 pp.; 1957

15. *Tropical Night Falling*　　Manuel Puig
Poignant last novel before the author's untimely death in
1990. Two elderly Argentinian sisters living in Rome gossip
about the people in their apartment complex.　　**192 pp.; 1991**

16. *Was*　　Geoff Ryman
Fantastic, if not exactly magical, politics emerge in his novels.
Ryman won the 1985 World Fantasy Award for holding up a
looking glass to it.　　**371 pp.; 1992**

17. *Beauty*　　Sheri Tepper
When her wicked aunt's curse is fulfilled on Beauty's six-
teenth birthday, she finds herself alone amid millions and millions of humans. Tepper is the author of *Raising the Stones*
and *Grass*, nominated for the Hugo Award.　　**412 pp.; 1991**

18. *The White Hotel*　　D. M. Thomas
Shortlisted for the Booker, this combines Freudian psychoan-
alytic ideas, the evil of modern history, and plenty of sex.
　　274 pp.; 1981

19. *The Hobbitt*   **J. R. R. Tolkien**
The doyen of the fantastic, the creator of Middle Earth—
where the language spoken is Elvish. *Lord of the Rings* is the
meal; *Hobbit* is dessert.   **312 pp.; 1974**

24

OTHER LANDS, OTHER VOICES

1. *Year of the Elephant*   Leila Abouzeid (Morocco)
This is the counterpoint to Paul Bowles's *The Sheltering Sky*.
She writes from the inside of a society that strictly limits
women, and makes Morocco seem a lot less trendy and inviting.   **129 pp.; 1989**

2. *Anthills of the Savannah*   Chinua Achebe (Nigeria)
By the author of *Things Fall Apart*, this view of modern
Africa uses the conflict between the city and tribal villages,
drought, and third world politics as background.
                                                216 pp.; 1988

3. *The War of the Saints*   Jorge Amado (Brazil)
Now in his late seventies, this author of twenty-one novels
(which have been translated into forty-six languages) writes
in his preface that he plans to tell "the small tale of Adalgisa
and Manela and a few other descendants of the love between
the Spaniard Francisco Romero Pérez y Pérez and Andreza da
Anunciaçao, the beautiful Andreza de Yansan, a dark mulatto
girl." And so he does. Lovers of magic realism will be thrilled.
                                                357 pp.; 1993

4. *Flaubert's Parrot*   Julian Barnes (Great Britain)
Barnes is a peculiar, quirky writer with a big following. This

book was followed by *The Porcupine* and preceded by *A History of the World in 10½ Chapters*. In *Talking It Over* Barnes deals with the familiar questions: what's real in fiction and who's in charge?   **190 pp.; 1985**

5. *Circle of Friends*   **Maeve Binchy (Ireland)**
Dublin in the 1950s and how women come of age in the land of writers. Binchy, a hugely popular author, wrote *Light a Penny Candle* and others.   **565 pp.; 1991**

6. *Possession*   **A. S. Byatt (Great Britain)**
In this modern version of a Victorian novel two academics research the lives of two poets; the story climaxes on a storm-tossed night in the churchyard where one of the poets is buried. This won England's Booker Prize.   **555 pp.; 1990**

7. *Mazurka for Two Dead Men*   **Camilo José Cela (Spain)**
Story of the Spanish Civil War, the death of "Lionheart" Gamuzo, and how he is avenged by his brother Tanis. For both events the blind accordion player Gaudencio plays the same mazurka. Cela won the Nobel Prize in 1989.

                                              272 pp.; 1992

 8. *Murther and Walking Spirits*   **Robertson Davies (Canada)**
The prolific Davies presents a murdered writer whose ghost relives his family's history on a movie screen. The critic who killed him is watching too.   **357 pp.; 1991**

9. *The Radiant Way*   **Margaret Drabble (Great Britain)**
This tenth novel, which begins on December 31, 1979, is the story of three Englishwomen. We follow them for the next five years, as the 1970s give way to the 1980s and the world changes around them.   **408 pp.; 1987**

10. *The House on Moon Lake*   **Francesca Duranti (Italy)**
This third Duranti book won the Bagutta, Martina Franca, and City of Milan prizes. This is the story of Garrone, who translates an obscure novel, and how that act rewards and menaces his own existence. It was followed by *Happy Ending* and *Personal Effects*, a favorite of mine.   **181 pp.; 1986**

11. *The Rape of Shavi*   Buchi Emecheta (Nigeria)
Set partly in an imaginary country by the edge of the African
Sahara and partly in England, this is a portrait of a people
confronted for the first time with the ways of the civilized
world.   178 pp.; 1983

12. *Ruin*   Beppe Fenoglio (Italy)
A seminal work of Italian neorealism by someone widely considered to be one of the most influential Italian writers of the
twentieth century. Fenoglio lived from 1922 to 1963.
                                                      94 pp.; 1992

13. *A State of Siege*   Janet Frame (New Zealand)
Malfred Signal returns to an idyllic island after her mother
dies. Terror reigns on the first night when an intruder pounds
on the door and the still-unconnected telephone does not
work. As in all of her work, the place under siege is really the
inner landscape of the human heart.   246 pp.; 1966

14. *Family Sayings*   Natalia Ginzburg (Italy)
Novel that relies on Ginzburg's memory and her evocation of
the past, particularly of her youth in Turin, where she was
raised as an atheist. (Her mother was Catholic, her father
Jewish.) She married Leone Ginzburg, who died in prison in
1944 after imprisonment by the fascists. Ginzburg wrote *The
Manzoni Family* in 1983.   181 pp.; 1967

15. *Requiem*   Shizuko Go (Japan)
Often called the Japanese *Diary of Anne Frank*, this novel
tells the story of a girl whose parents, brother, and friends are
killed in World War II. War, as always, remains futile.
                                                     122 pp.; 1992

16. *My Son's Story*   Nadine Gordimer (South Africa)
A Nobel Prize–winning author writes here of a "colored"
antiapartheid activist and the white woman he loves. *July's
People* is recommended too.   277 pp.; 1990

17. *Call of the Toad*   Günter Grass (Germany)
Considered by many to be Germany's greatest living writer,

the author of *The Tin Drum* writes here about middle-aged love, German and Polish schemes, and capitalism run amok.

248 pp.; 1992

18. *The Grisly Wife*   **Rodney Hall (Australia)**
Completes a trilogy, including *The Second Bridegroom* and *Captivity Captive*, this time focusing on women, especially Catherine Byrne, a nineteenth-century missionary who moves from England to Australia with "her nut-case prophet husband and his band of 8 female true believers, called by him the Household of Hidden Stars" (*New York Times*).

261 pp.; 1993

19. *Too Loud a Solitude*   **Bohumil Hrabil (Czechoslovakia)**
For thirty-five years Hant'a rescues books from the jaws of the hydraulic press before he compacts the trash. This baroque tale celebrates the indestructibility of the spoken word. Hrabil wrote *Closely Watched Trains* and *I Served the King of England*.

98 pp.; 1990

20. *My Life as a Dog*   **Reidar Jonsson (Sweden)**
The first novel about a parentless boy in a trilogy by this Swedish writer. In *My Father, His Son*, the second novel, Jonsson follows Ingemar Johansson into adulthood, the merchant marines, and his troubled marriage.   **201 pp.; 1990**

21. *The Metamorphosis*   **Franz Kafka (Czechoslovakia)**
Even if you read this one in college, a great discussion can evolve from why Gregor Samsa awakens one morning to find himself not a man but a giant insect.   **65 pp.; 1946**

22. *The Unbearable Lightness*   **Milan Kundera**
     of Being   **(Czechoslovakia)**
Tomas, a surgeon, Tereza, a dependable woman, Sabina, a freespirited artist, and her good-hearted lover Franz—all exist in a world shaped by irrevocable choices, fortuitous events, and plenty of sex. As the cynics say, be careful what you ask for.   **314 pp.; 1984**

23. *Palace of Desire:*　　　　Naguib Mahfouz (Egypt)
　The Cairo Trilogy II
A Nobel Prize–winning author writes about the emergence of
Egypt from colonization.　　　　　　　　　　**422 pp.; 1991**

24. *Beginning with My Streets*　　Czeslaw Milosz (Poland)
These are essays and recollections about time, religion, sin,
and friendship from the 1980 Nobel Laureate in literature.
　　　　　　　　　　　　　　　　　　　　288 pp.; 1992

25. *The Trench*　　　　Abdalrahman Munif (Lebanon)
The second volume of the *Cities of Salt* trilogy, this novel
chronicles the life of a fictional Arab town as it is transformed by the discovery of oil.　　　　　　**554 pp.; 1991**

26. *Hardboiled Wonderland*　　Haruki Murakami (Japan)
　and the End of the World
Murakami's hero is Ben Johnson, the cowboy turned character actor who "played in all those great John Ford movies."
As *Newsweek* said, "Pop culture references are like Popeye's
spinach in Murakami's fiction. It's hard to believe this was
written by a Japanese and easy to believe that he lives in the
USA now."　　　　　　　　　　　　　　**400 pp.; 1991**

27. *A Bend in the River*　　V. S. Naipul (born in Trinidad)
This is a chillingly accurate portrait of Africa in decay. Also
The Enigma of Arrival.　　　　　　　　　　**354 pp.; 1979**

28. *To Know a Woman*　　　　　　Amos Oz (Israel)
A retired Israeli secret service officer struggles to understand
his mother, mother-in-law, daughter, and his dead wife.
　　　　　　　　　　　　　　　　　　　　262 pp.; 1991

29. *The White Castle*　　　　Orhan Pamuk (Turkey)
This is the first of his four novels to be translated into
English; the narrator, a slave and former scholar who lives in
Constantinople in the final days of the Ottoman Empire,
teaches a man who is his physical double.　　**161 pp.; 1991**

30. *A Violent Life*　　　　Pier Paolo Pasolini (Italy)
This novel explores the brutal world of a young thief who is
eventually transformed.　　　　　　　　　　**320 pp.; 1959**

31. *Caetana's Sweet Song*   Nélida Piñon (Brazil)
The second of her eight novels to appear in English, this picaresque novel contains a multitude of self-deluded questers. The novel is set in 1970, during Brazil's military dictatorship.
                                                   402 pp.; 1992

32. *Sicilian Uncles*   Leonardo Sciascia (Italy)
Four novellas, all ironic political thrillers, by one of Italy's best writers.   205 pp.; 1986

33. *Cracking India*   Bapsi Sidhwa (Pakistan)
An eight-year-old girl is caught up in the partition of India in 1947. This novel is at once heartbreaking and funny.
                                                   289 pp.; 1991

34. *Ake: The Years of Childhood*   Wole Soyinka (Nigeria)
Although best known as a Nobel Prize–winning playwright, Soyinka has written in many genres, including fiction.
                                                   230 pp.; 1981

35. *The Eye of the Storm*   Patrick White (Australia)
White won the Nobel Prize shortly after publication of this novel. It focuses on the last weeks of an elderly woman who reminisces about her life and the tranquillity she experienced fifteen years earlier when she was temporarily stranded on an island.   608 pp.; 1973

36. *Mr. Mani*   A. B. Yehoshua (Israel)
Chronicles six generations in the Mani family from the mid-nineteenth century to the mid-1980s, beginning in the present and moving, as memory moves, back to the past. Yehoshua is also the author of *Five Seasons* and *A Late Divorce*, all recommended reading.   369 pp.; 1992

37. *Dear Departed*   Marguerite Yourcenar
                                            (born in Belgium)
This is the first volume of her ancestral trilogy, which omits any discussion of Yourcenar's homosexuality. However, if you think your family's history is some story, read this! Highly recommended. Also *That Mighty Sculptor, Time; Memoirs of Hadrian*, and *Two Lives and a Dream*.   346 pp.; 1991

25

MOTHERS AND DAUGHTERS

1. *Altered Loves*   **Terri Apter**
Subtitled *Mothers and Daughters During Adolescence*. Here's
some good news about this relationship!   **230 pp.; 1990**

2. *During the Reign of the Queen of Persia*   **Joan Chase**
Almost a cult novel among writers, this story of three generations of women and their farm in northern Ohio is told
through the collective point of view of four teenage girls.
215 pp.; 1983

3. *Dale Loves Sophie to Death*   **Robb Forman Dew**
Dinah Howells returns to her childhood hometown of
Enfield, Ohio, with her three young children; she comes to
understand what it means to be someone's child and about
many kinds of love. *Fortunate Lives* followed. **217 pp.; 1981**

4. *Mother Love*   **Candace Flynt**
The story of three sisters in North Carolina and the contra-
dictory relationship that each had with her passionate and
difficult mother, who has recently died.   **342 pp.; 1987**

5. *Hideous Kinky*   **Esther Freud**
Semiautobiographical first novel by an actress who is the
great-granddaughter of Sigmund Freud and the daughter of

the artist Lucien Freud. Told from a five-year-old's point of view as she and her sister are schlepped through Morocco in the 1960s by their nonconformist mother.   186 pp.; 1992

6. *A Mother and Two Daughters*   Gail Godwin
In the stormy late 1970s, three women, Cate, Lydia, and their mother, Nell, come together in a small North Carolina town after the death of Leonard Strickland, father and husband.
                                                     564 pp.; 1982

7. *Men and Angels*   Mary Gordon
Anne Foster, an art historian with two children, needs a live-in baby-sitter when her husband leaves for a year's fellowship in France. A religious fanatic named Laura enters their lives while Anne is herself drawn into the life of Caroline Watson, an artist who has been dead for forty-five years. Gordon is also the author of *Final Payments* and *The Company of Women*, both recommended.   239 pp.; 1985

8. *Fierce Attachments*   Vivian Gornick
A memoir of life in the Bronx and the fight for a daughter's independence. The third woman in the puzzle is Nettie, an attractive, confused widow who lives next door.
                                                     204 pp.; 1987

9. *In a Country of Mothers*   A. M. Homes
Really a psychological thriller, this novel is about a twenty-four-year-old daughter whose adoptive mother still calls her every night at 11:00 P.M. Her therapist, whose infant daughter was given up for adoption twenty-four years ago, is also a big part of her problem.   275 pp.; 1993

10. *Pride of Family*   Carole Ione
Subtitled *Four Generations of American Women of Color*, this nonfictional story of a clan of artistocratic black mothers and daughters includes a discussion of their multiple marriages, bad hair, good men, etc., in a black patrician world.
                                                     224 pp.; 1991

11. *Pigs in Heaven*   **Barbara Kingsolver**
Picks up where *The Bean Trees* left off when Taylor Greer, an outspoken hillbilly from Kentucky, finds an abused Native American child, whom she names Turtle, on the front seat of her Volkswagen. Good discussion can be generated by the position of the adoptive mother versus the tribal prerogative.
343 pp.; 1993

12. *The Mother Knot*   **Jane Lazarre**
Powerful autobiographical account of the shock and pain of childbirth, the transformation of identity, and the ensuing ambivalent feelings, including those of love.   **188 pp.; 1976**

13. *Ghost Dance*   **Carole Maso**
Maso's first novel is most centrally about disappearance—of the narrator Vanessa Turin's poet mother, Christine Wing, and of her father. The mythic feeling and evocative language are both beautiful. Also *Ava*.   **275 pp.; 1986**

14. *The Good Mother*   **Sue Miller**
A contemporary version of the age-old struggle between maternal and sexual love emerges when Leo Cutter, an artist, enters the world of Anna Dunlap and her daughter, Molly. Great book; skip the movie.   **310 pp.; 1986**

15. *A Mother's Love*   **Mary Morris**
This novel, by the author of *The Waiting Room* and *Nothing to Declare*, is a disturbing tale about the loneliness and fear Ivy Slovak experiences when she is alone in New York with her infant son and with the memories of the mother who deserted her when she was seven.   **287 pp.; 1993**

16. *Beloved*   **Toni Morrison**
One of America's best writers tells the post–Civil War story of an escaped slave, Sethe, who lives in a small house in Ohio with, among others, a disturbing, compelling intruder—perhaps the ghost of her daughter, Beloved. Also *Sula* and *The Bluest Eye*.   **275 pp.; 1987**

17. *The Beggar Maid* **Alice Munro**
Like all the other collections of Munro's short stories, *Lives of Girls and Women; Something I've Been Meaning to Tell You; The Progress of Love; Friend of My Youth*, this one can be read as a novel since the tales are interconnected.

210 pp.; 1979

18. *'night, Mother* **Marsha Norman**
Winner of the 1983 Pulitzer, this play centers on Jessie, who has decided to commit suicide, and her mother, Thelma, who realizes that she is powerless to prevent it.   **89 pp.; 1983**

19. *Housekeeping* **Marilynne Robinson**
Robinson's reputation continues to rest on this one novel. It is the story of the adolescent Ruth's journey to self-consciousness and of the ways she is alienated from her sister, Lucille, after their mother's suicide. Aunt Sylvie is an unforgettable nonconformist.   **219 pp.; 1980**

20. *Anywhere but Here* **Mona Simpson**
Not everyone (thankfully) has a mother who leaves her on the side of the road and then comes back with an offer of ice cream cones. Here Adele August drives from Wisconsin to California to make Ann into a child star "while [she is] still a child." Unforgettable portrait of a mother nobody wants.

406 pp.; 1986

21. *In My Mother's House* **Elizabeth Winthrop**
Three-generation story of buried secrets, the ghosts of memory, and the ways in which they impact on the Websters, particularly the women, strong New Englanders from the 1800s to the present.   **523 pp.; 1988**

26

FATHERS, SONS, AND BROTHERS

1. *A Death in the Family*   James Agee
A posthumously published novel about the death of his
father, when Agee was six, that won a Pulitzer Prize.

                                        318 pp.; 1957

2. *Moon Palace*   Paul Auster
The mesmerizing narrative of Marco Stanley Fogg, orphan
and child of the 1960s. It spans three generations and moves
from Manhattan (and the Chinese restaurant near Columbia
University for which the novel was named) to the West, while
Fogg searches for his father and the keys to his origin.

                                        307 pp.; 1989

3. *Gabriel's Lament*   Paul Bailey
Abandoned son of an irascible, annoying father idolizes the
mother who left him. But you have to read to the *very* end to
understand the secret here. I love this book and the rumina-
tions it offers on misplaced loyalty.   **331 pp.; 1987**

4. *Go Tell It on the Mountain*   James Baldwin
Baldwin took ten years to write this first novel in order to
make sense out of the relationship with the father he hated.
He "had to understand the forces, the experience, the life that

shaped him before I could grow up myself, before I could become a writer."   **191 pp.; 1953**

5. *The Brothers*   **Frederick Barthelme**
Bud is a restless teacher at a small-town college in Biloxi, Mississippi; his brother, Del, is a former public relations man who moves to his brother's town, falls in love with his brother's wife, and gets involved with a woman half his age who collects grotesque stories about death and mutilation.
                                        262 pp.; 1993

6. *Blue River*   **Ethan Canin**
Evokes the mythic theme of good brother, bad brother; written in spare, exacting prose. Beautiful.   **220 pp.; 1991**

7. *A Model World and Other Stories*   **Michael Chabon**
Following his first novel, *The Mysteries of Pittsburgh*, Chabon writes here about the coming of age of Nathan Shapiro and the emotional exchanges between fathers and sons.   **207 pp.; 1993**

8. *Body and Soul*   **Frank Conroy**
First novel by the fifty-seven-year-old head of the Iowa Writers' Workshop, who is also an accomplished pianist—like the child-prodigy character searching for a father figure in this novel. Conroy's memoir is *Stop-Time*.   **450 pp.; 1993**

9. *David Copperfield*   **Charles Dickens**
In this partly autobiographical story, all of David's troubles begin when his widowed mother, Clara, marries the villainous Edward Murdstone. His spiritual father, Mr. Micawber, foils the unctuous scoundrel Uriah Heep.   **845 pp.; 1849–1850**

10. *Loon Lake*   **E. L. Doctorow**
This depression-era tale takes place at a tycoon's hidden mountain estate. In an ironic twist of the Horatio Alger story, the poor hero, Joe Korzeniowski of Paterson, New Jersey, becomes Joseph Patterson Bennett, the rich man's adopted son and heir to Loon Lake. But he is corrupted, not empowered, by the money.   **258 pp.; 1980**

11. *The Brothers Karamazov*   Fyodor Dostoevsky

The tragedy is dominated by Father Zossima in this masterful story of religious faith and sordid crime. The struggle between the elder Karamazov and his oldest son, Dmitri, is over the father's mistress, Grushenka. Only the youngest Karamazov, Alyosha, triumphs over the rottenness that is a family tradition.   **483 pp.; 1949**

12. *Absalom, Absalom!*   William Faulkner

Faulkner explores the intricate family histories of the Sutpens, Compsons, Coldfields, Bons, and the Joneses. The four chapters recounting Quentin Compson's conversation with his father, Jason III, continue the story of a poor white man, Thomas Sutpen, whose dynasty building results in tragic ruin. This book is a favorite of reading clubs.   **313 pp.; 1936**

13. *Roots*   Alex Haley

Most of America watched the televised version of Haley's partly fictional account of his ancestors in Africa, and many of them began to think about the relationship of sons to fathers, missing or present. It was left to the feminist movement to reemphasize the links between sons and mothers.
688 pp.; 1976

14. *The Nick Adams Stories*   Ernest Hemingway

Largely autobiographical stories of a midwestern boy who is being taught to hunt and fish by his doctor-father. Read them not in the order of publication but in chronological order: "Indian Camp," "The Doctor and the Doctor's Wife," "The Killers," "Ten Indians," "The End of Something," "The Three-Day Blow," "The Battler," "Now I Lay Me," "A Way You'll Never Be," "Big Two-Hearted River," "Cross-Country Snow," and "Fathers and Sons."   **268 pp.; 1972**

15. *The Lies Boys Tell*   Lamar Herrin

In this first novel, winner of the Associated Writing Programs Award for the Novel, a dying Ed Reece calls home his estranged son to help him retrace the paths of his life. They travel familiar and strange routes on a journey of reconciliation that encompasses husbands and wives and the opposed camps of two generations during the Vietnam War.

267 pp.; 1991

16. *The Music Room*   Dennis McFarland

Fine first novel about Martin Lambert's search for answers to his brother Perry's death—a journey back through memory. The alcoholic mother is like few characters ever created in contemporary fiction. Don't miss this one.   275 pp.; 1990

17. *Death of a Salesman*   Arthur Miller

Although many book clubs do not read plays, Miller's Pulitzer Prize–winning drama is the story of the pathetic Willy Loman, struggling to achieve some dignity in a society that prefers betrayal, and his equally ineffective sons, Biff and Happy. It can be read alongside any of the books on this list.

104 pp.; 1949

18. *The Sailor Who Fell From*   Yukio Mishima
Grace with the Sea

A devotee of the Japanese samurai tradition, and of a Japan free from Western influence, Mishima took his own life in a ritual suicide. In this impressionistic novel a young boy secretly watches the sailor, soon to be his stepfather, make love to his mother. Suffice it to say, the wedding does not take place.   181 pp.; 1965

19. *Northern Lights*   Tim O'Brien

This novel focuses on two brothers, one of whom has served in Vietnam (like O'Brien) and returned to join the other in the northern Minnesota town where they grew up. The strongest section, really about understanding relationships, emerges when the brothers are lost during a skiing trip and struggle to survive in the wilderness.   356 pp.; 1975

20. *Zen and the Art of*   Robert Pirsig
Motorcycle Maintenance

If you lived through the 1960s, you've already read this auto-biographical and philosophical exploration, grafted onto a

motorcycle trip of a father and son going west from Minnesota.   412 pp.; 1974

21. *Fly-Fishing Through the*   Howell Raines
Midlife Crisis

Ostensibly a book about Raines's avocation, but more profoundly about his seven-year feud with his father and brother
and his relationship with his dead friend Dick Blalock.
                                           352 pp.; 1993

22. *East of Eden*   John Steinbeck

Classic brother story in which the ne'er-do-well survives the
shock of discovering his mother's profession, while the pure
and upright brother disintegrates when confronted with the
truth. *Journal of a Novel* describes the writing of this book.
                                           602 pp.; 1952

23. *Unto the Sons*   Gay Talese

The well-known journalist and novelist traces his heritage
from southern Italy to Ocean City, New Jersey, principally by
focusing on his father's life.   636 pp.; 1992

24. *Fathers and Sons*   Ivan Turgenev

Largely a novel about ideas, including an 1860s movement in
Russia called nihilism, this is also a classic tale of conflict
between a father's ideas and the iconoclasm and skepticism of
the son.   243 pp.; 1930

25. *Rabbit Is Rich*   John Updike

Won the National Book Award and was preceded by *Rabbit
Run* (1960), Updike's second novel, and *Rabbit Redux*, which
won the NBA in 1972. Followed, inevitably, by *Rabbit Is
Dead*. In this one Rabbit (Harry Angstrom), like America in
the 1970s, has peaked, and the person who is the locus of his
intimations on mortality is his son, the troubled Nelson, who
returns home after three years at Kent State University.
                                           467 pp.; 1982

26. *The Promise of Light*   Paul Watkins

A story about personal legacy and responsibility, his fourth novel concerns Ben Sheridan, a first-generation Irish-American who learns that the man who raised him was not his father. Watkins wrote *Night over Day* when he was twenty-three; it was shortlisted for the Booker Prize.   **271 pp.; 1993**

27. *The Solid Mandala*   **Patrick White**
The twins, mad, gentle Arthur and conventional, fearful Waldo, are the strongly contrasted brothers in this Jungian novel by the Australian winner of the Nobel Prize for literature who died in 1990. "What I could not accept at the time was the invitation to fly to Stockholm and receive the award in person. This refusal must remain incomprehensible to all those who don't understand my nature or my books." Also *The Tree of Life* and *Voss*.   **309 pp.; 1966**

28. *Silent Passengers*   **Larry Woiwode**
The *New York Times* says that "Woiwode's characters are mostly parents and children sorting through complicated relationships. . . ." In "Owen's Father" a son recovers memories by staring at a photograph.   **131 pp.; 1993**

27

POLITICS AS USUAL?

1. *The Dollmaker*   **Harriette Arnow**
One of the first books to represent Kentuckians as the valiant
people they are, this novel focuses on the confrontation
between the individual conscience and socioeconomic forces.
Arnow also wrote *Mountain Path* and *Hunter's Horn*.

$$\text{549 pp.; 1954}$$

2. *The Handmaid's Tale*   **Margaret Atwood**
Offred is a Handmaid in the republic of Gilead where Hand-
maids are valued only if their ovaries are healthy. A chilling
vision of the possible.   **395 pp.; 1986**

3. *City Life*   **Donald Barthelme**
Stories where Barthelme makes the point that "[America] is
the country of brain damage," the epitome of which emerges
in "Kierkegaard Unfair to Schlegel." Read his early collection, *Come Back, Dr. Caligari* (1964), too.   **168 pp.; 1970**

4. *Henderson the Rain King*   **Saul Bellow**
Eugene Henderson travels to Africa in the 1950s to find out
how to live. He causes plenty of trouble in the bargain, and as
usual with Bellow, women are a big part of his problem.

341 pp.; 1959

5. *The Road to Wellville* T. Coraghessan Boyle

A historical farce set in 1907 in Battle Creek, Michigan, where corn flakes inventor Dr. John Harvey Kellogg's world-famous sanatarium attracts a mix of health nuts and hustlers.

476 pp.; 1993

6. *Theory of War* **Joan Brady**

This novel, based on the true story of Brady's grandfather—a white man who was a slave in America—should be much better known. **257 pp.; 1993**

7. *Civil Wars* **Rosellen Brown**

One of those novels that other novelists talk about. Jessie and Teddy Carll, survivors of the civil rights movement and still living in the very deep South, are forced by a family disaster (just as their own marriage is falling apart) to take in two children brought up by hard-rock segregationist parents.

432 pp.; 1984

8. *Cathedral* **Raymond Carver**

Stories by one of America's best writers, now dead from the effects of alcoholism, in which drained and empty characters, usually undereducated and working-class, are trapped in loss, futility, and emptiness. *What We Talk About When We Talk About Love* is recommended too. **227 pp.; 1983**

9. *Life in the Iron Mills* **Rebecca Harding Davis**

Davis was one of the most prominent nineteenth-century U.S. writers of realist regional fiction; her son was Richard Harding Davis, the newspaperman. This piece was first published in an April 1861 issue of the *Atlantic Monthly* and brought back into public consciousness by Tillie Olsen in the 1980s. Very much worth reading. **174 pp.; 1972**

10. *White Noise* **Don DeLillo**

Jack Gladney teaches the history of Nazism at a small college in Middle America. Then an ominous "airborne toxic event"—a black cloud of lethal gaseous fumes released in an industrial accident—threatens to engulf the town.

326 pp.; 1985

11. *U.S.A.*   John Dos Passos
Trilogy consisting of *The 42nd Parallel* (1930), *1919* (1932),
and *The Big Money* (1936), the quintessential political record
for those who are from immigrant backgrounds and are interested in the incorporation of European modernism into
American fiction.   *The 42nd Parallel*, 365 pp.;
                            1919, 412 pp.; *The Big Money*, 494 pp.

12. *Been Down So Long*   Richard Farina
   It Looks Like Up to Me
An antiheroic comedy that spotlights the banality Farina finds
at the heart of civilization. The setting is Cornell, seen
through his prism.   329 pp.; 1966

13. *PrairyErth*   William Least Heat-Moon
This intensive look at a 744-square-mile piece of America
(Chase County, Kansas) by the author of *Blue Highways* is an
antidote to pollution and environmental corruption. As Heat-
Moon writes, "the land, like a good library, lets a fellow
extend himself, stretch time . . . slip the animal bondage of
the perpetual present. . . . If a traveler can get past the barri-
ers of ignorance and forgetfulness, a journey into the land is a
way into some things and a way out of others." Amen.
                                                648 pp.; 1990

14. *The Ivory Swing*   Janette Turner Hospital
Winner of Canada's Seal Award in 1982, this novel, set in
India, presents a woman's pivotal moment of struggle and
self-recognition and is a poignant story of an outsider who
temporarily intersects with an alien world. Hospital's short
story collections, *Dislocations* and *Isobars*, are strongly recommended, as is *The Last Magician*.   252 pp.; 1982

15. *The Hotel New Hampshire*   John Irving
In this novel Irving handles teenage rape, terrorist violence,
and incest, all social problems that have a political genesis.
The World According to Garp catapulted him to international fame.   401 pp.; 1981

16. *Among Schoolchildren*   Tracy Kidder
The nonfiction chronicle of one teacher's passionate dedication to the children in her classroom and a clear look at what is wrong with many others.   **340 pp.; 1989**

17. *The Book of Laughter*   Milan Kundera
   and Forgetting
Kundera often appears not only as the author but as a character in his own fiction, and his autobiography becomes the political history of postwar Czechoslovakia. He asks a good question: how does any person live today? Answer: by laughter and forgetting.   **228 pp.; 1980**

18. *Harlot's Ghost*   Norman Mailer
Very long novel full of real and imaginary people and a good look at current events through the eyes of three aristocratic Yankees who work for the C.I.A.   **1,328 pp.; 1991**

19. *Karma Cola*   Gita Mehta
This first book, a nonfiction work written in three weeks, satirizes the Western search for the wisdom of the East.
                    201 pp.; 1979

20. *No Other Life*   Brian Moore
A fictionalized account of Father Aristide's messianic rise and fall from power in Haiti.   **223 pp.; 1993**

21. *Animal Farm*   George Orwell
World-famous allegory in which the animals, and the rest of us, learn that not all pigs are trustworthy, nor are all animals created equal.   **155 pp.; 1954**

22. *Daughter of Earth*   Agnes Smedley
Dirt-hard proletarian feminist novel re-creates the story of a tireless political activist, in most ways Smedley herself, who emerged from poverty and a life as a tobacco stripper.
                    391 pp.; 1987

23. *Earth Abides*   George R. Stewart
As *The Christian Science Monitor* noted, this is "a provoca-

tive commentary on some of the most persistent dilemmas (racial, social & biological) which confront mankind." Here nature, order, and survival are all interrupted.   373 pp.; 1949

24. *Hollywood*   Gore Vidal
A novel, this is part of Vidal's so-called biography of the United States. It blends history and fiction, using the public lives of Hearst, Wilson, Elinor Glyn, and Chaplin. A great read.   437 pp.; 1990

25. *Slaughterhouse-Five*   Kurt Vonnegut
The hero goes to Dresden as it is about to be destroyed by the Allies, to Ilium (Ithaca, home of Cornell), and to the planet Tralfamadore. Vonnegut wrote, among others, *Cat's Cradle* and *God Bless You, Mr. Rosewater*.   215 pp.; 1969

26. *Philadelphia Fire*   John Edgar Wideman
Novel inspired by the 1985 bombing (ordered by the black mayor) of a Philadelphia row house occupied by black people in a cult called Move. Read *Brothers and Keepers* too.
                                                    208 pp.; 1990

28

QUESTIONING THE MIRACULOUS

1. *Baby of the Family*   Tina McElroy Ansa
From the moment of her birth in a rural black hospital in
Georgia, Lena McPherson, born with a caul over her face, is
recognized by all the nurses as a special child with the power
to see ghosts and predict the future.   **265 pp.; 1989**

2. *The Forms of Water*   Andrea Barrett
In this novel a retired monk escapes from a rest home. Barrett, a fine writer, also wrote *The Middle Kingdom*.
                                              292 pp.; 1993

3. *Giles Goat-Boy*   John Barth
Barth's writing reminds the reader of the boisterous tone of
Cervantes, and here the modern university is transformed into
a universe by an academic who has gone nuts. Is the book's
author a computer? Barth also wrote *Lost in the Funhouse*
and *Sabbatical*.   **710 pp.; 1966**

4. *Rebecca*   Daphne du Maurier
All about Manderley, the place where "the dead come back
and watch the living." Gothic suspense at its best.
                                              446 pp.; 1938

5. *Carmen Dog*   Carol Emshwiller

Hilarious radical version of housewives devolving into snarling mutts while their pets become more human and start helping out at home. The heroine, Pooch, runs away to New York (where else?) to become an opera singer.   **161 pp.; 1990**

6. *A Passage to India*   E. M. Forster

Forster's greatest novel is set in India and examines the relations between the English and the Indians in the early 1920s. The scenes near the caves and the death of Mrs. Moore both lead to great discussions about this topic heading.

322 pp.; 1924

7. *Constancia and Other*   Carlos Fuentes
   Stories for Virgins

Five magical novella-length stories by the Mexican writer concerning the eruption of the bizarre and uncanny in the lives of his characters.   **340 pp.; 1990**

8. *JR*   William Gaddis

The story of Das Rheingold, the dwarfish Alberich—a novel with Wagnerian overtones, but really about moneymaking, business, depersonalization, and an individual loss of recognition.   **725 pp.; 1975**

9. *One Hundred Years of Solitude*   Gabriel García Márquez

Written by one of our greatest living writers, this is the story of the rise, fall, birth, and death of the mystical town of Macondo, as seen through the history of the Buendia family.

422 pp.; 1970

10. *Black Narcissus*   Rumer Godden

A small band of nuns settles in the Himalayas, and they are disturbed either by the old fakir in the garden or by the mountain itself.   **294 pp.; 1939**

11. *Mariette in Ecstasy*   Ron Hansen

Bestselling story of a young postulant's claim to divine possession and religious ecstasy in a small convent in upstate New York over a quarter century ago. Lots of questions for the reader to answer.   **192 pp.; 1991**

12. *Steppenwolf*   **Hermann Hesse**
In Hesse's best-known novel, the protagonist Harry Haller is introduced into the Magic Theatre—a fantastic realm devoted to liberating the senses—by Hermine, a free-spirited androgyne. Those interested in Eastern philosophy will like *Siddhartha*.   **309 pp.; 1929**

13. *Carmichael's Dog*   **R. M. Koster**
World-famous author of successful science fiction tetralogy is possessed by the demons of lust, envy, sloth, avarice, wrath, and, especially, pride.   **320 pp.; 1992**

14. *The Hour of the Star*   **Clarice Lispector**
This last postmodern novel by the Brazilian short story writer and novelist is about the socioeconomic problems of a naive, proletarian girl. Lispector is known for first-person, stream-of-consciousness, epiphanic moments.   **96 pp.; 1986**

15. *Feather Crowns*   **Bobbie Ann Mason**
Fire-and-brimstone revival meetings, quintuplets, and death, all in Kentucky, where Mason lives. An American parable with universal resonances.   **454 pp.; 1993**

16. *Song of Solomon*   **Toni Morrison**
One of America's best novelists in a tour de force about mystical flights, shamans, mother love, and the power of myth. The scene where Milkman Dead visits his mother's grave is unforgettable.   **341 pp.; 1978**

17. *The Flight from the Enchanter*   **Iris Murdoch**
Not surprising (since Murdoch was an Oxford don) that one critic described this novel as "a very brainy fairy tale," and another said it was a "modern *Nightmare Abbey*." Thoroughly enjoyable and much better than Murdoch's later novels.   **316 pp.; 1956**

18. *The Witching Hour*   **Anne Rice**
Rowan Mayfair, a San Francisco neurosurgeon who brings a drowned man back to life, is descended from witches. The setting is Rice's actual house in the Garden District of New

Orleans. In *Lasher* the queen of the coven flees the demon whom she hates but finds irresistible.   **965 pp.; 1990**

19. *Frankenstein*   **Mary Shelley**
Let's get it straight: Frankenstein is the *scientist*! He's the one who creates the "hideous progeny," last seen as he traveled across the frozen shore to loose havoc on the world.

192 pp.; 1818

20. *Various Miracles*   **Carol Shields**
Marvelous short stories, including "Mrs. Turner Cutting the Grass," by one of the finest writers living in Canada. In *The Republic of Love* two unlikely people in Winnipeg, a folklorist studying mermaids and a radio deejay on the graveyard shift, stumble into the territory of the title. *Swann*, a novel, is recommended too.   **183 pp.; 1985**

21. *Memento Mori*   **Muriel Spark**
A collection of London grotesques between the ages of seventy and one hundred, all of them old friends or acquaintances, get the same phone message from an unidentified caller. The voice says, "Remember You Must Die." This is comedy, combined with tragedy, at its best.   **224 pp.; 1959**

22. *Dracula*   **Bram Stoker**
As "the whole man" crawled down the castle wall, what could the reader think? "What manner of man—or creature—is this?"   **382 pp.; 1897**

23. *The Cloning of Joanna May*   **Fay Weldon**
Joanna May discovers that her ex-husband, Carl May, nuclear entrepreneur extraordinaire, had secretly arranged thirty years ago for four clones of her to be produced from an extracted egg. All of Weldon's books are recommended; she is smart, socially perceptive, and usually way ahead of her time.

265 pp.; 1989

24. *The Invisible Man*   **H. G. Wells**
A mad scientist concocts a potion that makes him invisible;

then he begins to terrorize the inhabitants of a small town. So, how'd he do it? And why?   **235 pp.; 1897**

25. *Sister Water*   Nancy Willard
The angel of death, a cat named The Everpresent Fullness, the Buddha Uproar Cafe, an indoor stream where fish swim into view and then vanish under the floor—*no one* does magical essences better than Willard.   **255 pp.; 1993**

29

ATTENTION, WOMEN

1. *Womenfolks: Growing Up Down South*   **Shirley Abbott**
Much more than a memoir, this is also a meditation on family myth and tradition, and a fine look at the gritty, independent women of this region.   **224 pp.; 1983**

2. *The Jewish Woman*   **Charlotte Baum, Paula Hyman,**
     in America   **Sonya Michel**
Here is the struggle to establish the family in the New World, care for newcomers, protect immigrant girls from pimps, and endure the sweatshops. The authors even deal with the "Yid-dishe Mamma" and the guilt merchants produced by Philip Roth et al.   **261 pp.; 1976**

3. *Iron John*   **Robert Bly**
At least here the men pass the drum instead of the ammuni-tion. Bly explains why men need to lighten up, smell the flow-ers, visit the forest primeval, and develop initiation rituals for themselves. His real goal is to discuss mentors and the hunger of men for fathers.   **268 pp.; 1990**

4. *Written by Herself*   **Jill Ker Conway (editor)**
An anthology of autobiographies of American women from

Jane Addams to Maxine Hong Kingston, many of whom invented their own lives. **656 pp.; 1992**

5. *The Second Sex* — Simone de Beauvoir
One of the two first major texts of feminist criticism. (The other was Woolf's *A Room of One's Own*, see no. 26.) De Beauvoir offers, according to the critic Catharine R. Stimpson, "a systematic analysis, derived from existential philosophy, of the facts about the totality of women's condition [and] the instrument of reason to assemble it." **732 pp.; 1949**

6. *Women Who Run with the Wolves* — Clarissa P. Estes
Myths and folk tales reinterpreted by a Jungian analyst. Stayed on the *New York Times* bestseller list for months. Interesting and new. **520 pp.; 1992**

7. *Sexual Violence:* — Linda A. Fairstein
Our War Against Rape
The Chief of the Sex Crimes Prosecution Unit in the Manhattan District Attorney's office begins with an account of the 1985 New York City rapes by the man who became known as the Midtown Rapist. She has also been involved in prosecuting the Robert Chambers Preppy Murder Trial (1986) and the case of the Central Park Jogger (1989). So, *before* you buy Roiphe's comments about hysteria on American campuses, read *this* book. **288 pp.; 1993**

8. *Backlash* — Susan Faludi
Inestimable and thorough analysis of the ways in which society has conspired to devalue the accomplishments of feminism. *Required* reading no matter which side you are on.
552 pp.; 1991

9. *The Women's Room* — Marilyn French
A groundbreaking fictional account of a whole generation of women. A good discussion can be generated about what (if anything) has changed in the lives of women today.
687 pp.; 1977

ninine Mystique   **Betty Friedan**
r of feminism explains why so many women were
lousy for so long. Her new book, *The Fountain of*
to put a happy face on aging.   **410 pp.; 1963**

11. *In a Different Voice*   Carol Gilligan

Groundbreaking work about female moral development and the female life cycle. She examines the qualities defined as women's weaknesses and shows them to be strengths. *Making Connections* is interesting too.   **174 pp.; 1982**

12. *Writing a Woman's Life*   Carolyn Heilbrun

The distinguished critic (also the mystery writer Amanda Cross) discusses three ways that women talk about their own lives: in autobiography, in fiction, or as biography. A useful, important book.   **131 pp.; 1988**

13. *Yearning*   bell hooks

Subtitled *Race, Gender, and Cultural Politics*, this book explores the social conditions, feminism, and sex roles among African-Americans from 1975 to 1990. Good bibliography.
    236 pp.; 1990

14. *Toward a Feminist*   Catherine MacKinnon
Theory of the State

Katie Roiphe calls MacKinnon "the Antiporn Star" for her crusade against pornographic images of women, a view with which I would largely disagree. So, take four aspirins and consider reading MacKinnon, Roiphe, and Fairstein for the same reading club meeting. And good luck.   **330 pp.; 1989**

15. *Listen to Their Voices*   Mickey Pearlman

Essay interviews with writing women from Jane Smiley to Fay Weldon about childhood, religion, memory, and the phenomenon of the hyphenated (i.e., Chinese-, African-, or Filipina-) writer in America. Also *A Voice of One's Own*—for Joyce Carol Oates, Rosellen Brown, and more—and *Between Friends*.   **224 pp.; 1992**

16. *Lives on the Edge*   Valerie Polakow

Subtitled *Single Mothers and Their Children in the Other America*. Polakow reviews the abuse, neglect, and exploitation of children in the eighteenth and nineteenth centuries and reminds us that in 1989, 52 percent of families in poverty were headed by women (up from 23 percent in 1959) and that a single mother in a minimum-wage job earns 20 percent less than what is defined as a poverty-level income for a family of three. My advice: get beyond race and think gender.

222 pp.; 1993

17. *The Morning After: Sex, Fear,*   Katie Roiphe
    and Feminism on Campus

Much, in my view, to disagree with re Roiphe's naive take on date rape and politically correct feminism. However, take (at least) two aspirins and have the discussion. Fairstein is a good antidote. See MacKinnon.   180 pp.; 1993

18. *First Nights*   Susan Fromberg Schaeffer

Two women—Anna Asta (based on Greta Garbo) and Ivy Cook, her companion and maid—are polar opposites but bound through love and the similarities in the experience of all women.   640 pp.; 1993

19. *Sassafras, Cypress, and Indigo*   Ntozake Shange

Focuses on women's alternatives in their relationships with men in this mix of fiction, poetry, songs, letters, recipes.

224 pp.; 1982

20. *Man Made Language*   Dale Spender

In *Women of Ideas and What Men Have Done to Them* Spender wrote that women are "producing knowledge which is often different from that produced by men, in a society controlled by men. If they like what we produce they will appropriate it, if they can use what we produce (even against us) they will take it, if they do not want to know, they will lose it. But rarely, if ever, will they treat us as they treat their own." That about sums it up.   250 pp.; 1985

21. *Revolution From Within*   Gloria Steinem
A founding mother of feminism in America talks about her
own and everyone else's struggle to achieve self-esteem.
                                                377 pp.; 1991

22. *You Just Don't Understand*   Deborah Tannen
Now we know for sure: men and women don't speak the
same language. (What a surprise!) Women as a group value
intimacy over independence, while men choose the reverse
formula—at least according to Tannen.   330 pp.; 1990

23. *Possessing the Secret of Joy*   Alice Walker
The aftermath of the painful ritual clitoridectomy agreed to
by Tashi, a black African woman who has appeared in other
Walker novels, almost destroys her life.   286 pp.; 1992

24. *Black-Eyed Susans/*   Mary Helen Washington
      Midnight Birds
Subtitled *Stories by and About Black Women*, this collection
also includes good biographical and critical overviews on
Gwendolyn Brooks, Gayl Jones, Alice Walker, Toni Cade
Bambara, and others.   398 pp.; 1975

25. *The Beauty Myth*   Naomi Wolf
As you may have noticed, standards of beauty tend to devalue
and oppress women; the question is, to what extent? In *Fire
With Fire* Wolf argues that the women's movement has sabo-
taged itself with its emphasis on victimization. You can get a
good discussion out of either one.   352 pp.; 1991

26. *A Room of One's Own*   Virginia Woolf
In this 1929 bible of many writing women, Woolf discusses
women's subjugation, women and fiction, and the possibilities offered by androgyny. Most literary historians would
agree that this is the first major achievement of feminist crti-
cism in the English language.   199 pp.; 1929

30

BE A SPORT

1. *Punch Lines*   **Phil Berger**
Berger formerly wrote about boxing for the *New York Times*,
and these are magazine and newspaper articles published over
the last twenty-five years.   **328 pp.; 1993**

2. *Friday Night Lights*   **H. G. Bissinger**
This one is as much about small-town life in Odessa, Texas,
and the struggle between sports and education, as it is about
football.   **364 pp.; 1990**

3. *Ball Four*   **Jim Bouton**
Twenty years ago Bouton blew the whistle on baseball as a
clean, all-American sport. Still a great read.   **400 pp.; 1970**

4. *Blue Ruin*   **Brendan Boyd**
Want to know what really happened during the notorious
1919 World Series between the Chicago White Sox and the
Cincinnati Reds?   **352 pp.; 1991**

5. *Dogleg Madness*   **Mike Bryan**
Believe it or not, a good book on golf! Herbert Warren Wind
writes well about this sport too.   **228 pp.; 1988**

6. *When the Game Was Black and White*   **Bruce Chadwick**
Subtitled *The Illustrated History of Baseball's Negro Leagues*,

this impressive collection of photos, with text, is by the *New York Daily News* sportswriter.   204 pp.; 1992

7. *A Season on the Brink*   **John Feinstein**
There's plenty to say about the notorious University of Indiana coach Bobby Knight. For those who are still mystified, Feinstein explains how he wins and why his players are loyal.
311 pp.; 1986

8. *Handful of Summers*   **Gordon Forbes**
A good book about tennis players, South Africa, and one man's biography.   238 pp.; 1979

9. *The Breaks of the Game*   **David Halberstam**
The writer spends a year with the Portland NBA team and the famed Bill Walton. Halberstam's book on Olympic crew, *The Contenders*, is also recommended.   362 pp.; 1981

10. *Dock Ellis in the Country of Baseball*   **Donald Hall and Dock Ellis**
Profile of the gifted pitcher by the noted essayist, poet, and baseball fanatic.   254 pp.; 1976

11. *Bang the Drum Slowly*   **Mark Harris**
Fantastic baseball novel from the 1950s; made into the best baseball movie ever with Robert De Niro and Michael Moriarty. *The Southpaw* is the sequel.   243 pp.; 1956

12. *Muhammed Ali*   **Thomas Hauser**
A moving and probing oral history–type portrait of the most popular man in the world.   544 pp.; 1991

13. *Beyond a Boundary*   **C. L. R. James**
Good read on the West Indies, black-white relations, the legacies of the British Empire, and cricket. Some beautiful writing here by the famous Marxist historian and critic.
255 pp.; 1963

14. *Shoeless Joe*   **W. P. Kinsella**
Kinsella's novel was later reissued as *Field of Dreams* after

the baseball movie of that name was made. "Build it and they will come" has entered the vocabulary.   **265 pp.; 1982**

15. *Sportsworld*   **Robert Lipsyte**
Unsurpassed, if cynical, essays about America's obsession with pro sports from the seasoned *New York Times* reporter. Especially brilliant on Mohammed Ali. Also recommended is his bestselling young adult novel, *The Contender*, about a young black boxer.   **292 pp.; 1975**

16. *The Natural*   **Bernard Malamud**
Much sadder than the movie with Robert Redford and in all ways a truer story about baseball.   **237 pp.; 1952**

17. *Jim Murray: An Autobiography*   **Jim Murray**
Pulitzer Prize–winning columnist for the *Los Angeles Times* writes about Michael Jordan and many others, but the parts about his own childhood and family in Hartford are sweetest.   **268 pp.; 1993**

18. *On Boxing*   **Joyce Carol Oates**
Evolved from a philosophical essay on the sport of boxing for the *New York Times*. Boxing also dominates her novel, *You Must Remember This*.   **118 pp.; 1987**

19. *Mortal Stakes*   **Robert B. Parker**
Parker writes the Spenser mysteries about the Boston detective, and this one is about baseball, women with pasts, and the Mob. Terrific.   **172 pp.; 1975**

20. *Only the Ball Was White*   **Robert Peterson**
Here's a good read about the Negro Leagues of baseball in the 1920s and 1930s.   **406 pp.; 1970**

21. *The Glory of Their Times*   **Larry Ritter**
This is a classic—and, as subtitled, the *Story of the Early Days of Baseball Told by the Men Who Played It*, and compiled by Ritter. Interesting on baseball players of the 1920s and 1930s.   **360 pp.; 1966**

22. *Papa Jack*   **Randy Roberts**
You can rent a video of *Great White Hope* after you've read this book about the boxer Jack Johnson.   **274 pp.; 1983**

23. *Second Wind*   **Bill Russell and Taylor Branch**
Opinionated, sometimes scary memoir by basketball's big man. Taylor Branch is the author of *Parting the Waters*.

265 pp.; 1979

24. *Almost Famous*   **David Small**
This is a small, dark novel about baseball and frustration.

416 pp.; 1982

25. *Heaven Is a Playground*   **Dick Telander**
Telander writes about inner-city kids on the basketball courts, aiming for the NBA.   **282 pp.; 1976**

26. *The Appearance of Impropriety*   **Walter Walker**
A murder mystery about basketball, blackmail, and murder. Colin Cromwell, a sportswriter in the San Francisco Bay area, attempts to document the goings-on in the NBA's latest expansion team, the Golden Gaters. Greedy owners, out-of-control managers, and agents; pro ball today!   **336 pp.; 1993**

31

KID STUFF

1. *Sounder*   **William H. Armstrong**
Courage and love bind a black family despite prejudice and
inhumanity in the Deep South.   **136 pp.; 1969**

2. *The Indian in the Cupboard*   **Lynn Reid Banks**
A nine-year-old boy receives a plastic Indian, a cupboard, and
a little key for his birthday. When he finds himself involved in
adventure, the Indian comes to life and befriends him. Also
The Secret of the Indian.   **181 pp.; 1980**

3. *Cherokee Bat and the Goat Guys*   **Francesca Lia Block**
As she did in *Weetzie Bat* and *Witch Baby*, Block creates an
idiosyncratic version of Los Angeles. Cherokee, her "almost-
sister" Witch Baby, Raphael and Angel Juan (two other members of the Goat Guys, a rock band) all get magical costumes
which have a very bad influence on them—eventually and
thankfully dispelled.   **128 pp.; 1992**

4. *Blubber*   **Judy Blume**
The *New York Times* called *Blubber* an Outstanding Book of
the Year twenty years ago, and it remains so today. Linda's
weight problems inspire the cruel instincts of the mob in her
fellow fifth graders, and any child who feels victimized will
love this one. Blume is famous for *Are You There, God? It's*

Me, Margaret; Then Again, Maybe I Won't; Otherwise Known as Sheila the Great; Tales of a Fourth Grade Nothing, and *Iggie's House*.   **153 pp.; 1974**

5. *The Secret Garden*   **Frances H. Burnett**
When the young orphan Mary Lennox arrives on the Yorkshire moors from India, she makes discoveries about what illness means and how sad some secrets can be. A classic for all ages. (In this house we've worn out about eight copies!)
375 pp.; 1911

6. *The Pinballs*   **Betsy Byars**
Although this engaging novel about kids sent to a foster home was an American Library Association Notable Children's Book fifteen years ago, the subject matter of young people without viable parents is even more prevalent today. Also *Summer of the Swans* and *The Seven Treasure Hunts*
136 pp.; 1977

7. *A Hero Ain't Nothin' but a Sandwich*   **Alice Childress**
Benjie is today's thirteen-year-old with a monkey on his back—in this case heroin. But he is also a funny, courageous kid about whom the reader cares.   **126 pp.; 1973**

8. *The Chocolate War*   **Robert Cormier**
A classic in which a high school freshman discovers what happens when he arouses the wrath of the school bullies. *The Bumblebee Flies Anyway* is a young adult mystery; Barney wonders why he is the control subject in an experimental clinic.   **253 pp.; 1974**

9. *The Witches*   **Roald Dahl**
Modern classic about a young boy and his Norwegian grandmother, an expert on witches, who together foil a witches' plot to destroy the world's children by turning them into mice.   **201 pp.; 1985**

10. *The Cat Ate My Gymsuit*   **Paula Danziger**
An all-time favorite about the bored Marcy Lewis, her tyrannical father, the usual fears about weight and acne, and the

good English teacher, Ms. Finney, who creates an uproar over her refusal to pledge allegiance to the flag. Danziger wrote *The Pistachio Prescription* and *Can You Sue Your Parents for Malpractice?*   147 pp.; 1974

11. *Hardy Boys Casefiles,*   Franklin Dixon
  Case 75, No Way Out

See comments on Nancy Drew. In this one Rob Niles is a master of the wilderness sport of orienteering. But he's in trouble on this trip, and the Hardy boys, Frank and Joe, have to use their survival skills to avoid the rattlesnakes, rock slides, and sniper fire. All the stories have been updated.

                                     154 pp.; reprint 1993

12. *Morning Girl*   Michael Dorris

A truer, more honest look at Columbus's arrival through the eyes of a girl, Morning Girl, and her younger brother, Star Boy, both growing up in 1492 on a Bahamian island. Dorris also wrote *A Yellow Raft in Blue Water*.   74 pp.; 1992

13. *Nobody's Family Is Going to Change*   Louise Fitzhugh

Eleven-year-old Emma wants to become a lawyer; her seven-year-old brother wants to be a dancer. The message here is that children must take the initiatives for their own lives since parents are often stuck in old ideas.   221 pp.; 1974

14. *Asterix and Caesar's Gift*   Rene de Goscinny;
                                   drawings by M. Uderzo

My own daughter took her Asterix books with her when she left for college. These are sophisticated picture books with text (they look something like cartoons), often full of puns, wordplay, information about culture, history, and language. Since they are imported, they are often a bit more expensive than the usual books for kids, but worth it in every sense; several volumes come in Latin (*Asterix Apud Brittannos*, etc.), French, and other languages. *Asterix and Cleopatra*, *Asterix and the Golden Sickle*, *Asterix in Belgium* are some of the other volumes.   48 pp.; 1977

15. *Your Old Pal, Al*   Constance C. Greene

Al is a twelve-year-old girl whose father has just remarried. On top of that, her best friend has just invited sophisticated Polly to stay with her for two weeks. Greene is best known for *A Girl Called Al*, *I Know You, Al*, and *Al(exandra) the Great*.   **149 pp.; 1979**

16. *Dustland*   Virginia Hamilton

Part of a trilogy: Volume 1 is *Justice*, Volume 2 is *Dustland*, and Volume 3 is *The Gathering*. Four children, all possessing extraordinary mental powers, are projected far into the future to a bleak region called Dustland.   **180 pp.; 1980**

17. *Words of Stone*   Kevin Henkes

Two lonely children in rural Wisconsin become friends one summer. This is a book about kinship and betrayal by the author of *Chrysanthemum* and *The Zebra Wall*.

160 pp.; 1992

18. *Tintin in Tibet*   Hergé

No child who likes to read and loves mysteries should grow up without the Tintin books; hold on to them because they will no doubt be collectors' items. Most editions are also available in French. *Tintin's Moon Adventures*, *Land of Black Gold*, *Destination Moon*, *The Castafiore Emerald*, *Valley of the Cobras*, and many more books are available.

62 pp.; 1975

19. *The Outsiders*   S. E. Hinton

Three brothers struggle to stay together after their parents' death. Great book about establishing identity among the conflicting values of adolescent society.   **188 pp.; 1967**

20. *Ooh-la-la (Max in Love)*   Maira Kalman

Thousands of adults have been caught sneaking into the kids' section of bookstores nationwide. Here are the Parisian adventures of Max Stravinsky, Kalman's dog-poet. The illustrations are marvelous. Don't miss *Sayonara, Mrs. Kackelman* either.   **unpaged; 1991**

21. *Nancy Drew Files, Case 82,*   **Carolyn Keene**
    Dangerous Relations

No list for kids can be without Nancy Drew, now fifty years in print. All of them have been completely updated, and even the most reluctant reader will get hooked on these. And guess what! A single parent, a father (yet!), is raising her, and the family is not *dysfunctional* or on welfare!

                                     154 pp.; reprint 1993

22. *Eli's Songs*   **Monte Killingsworth**

A twelve-year-old boy from Los Angeles is sent to live with relatives in rural Oregon and takes solace in a nearby forest that is eventually threatened by loggers. Unbelievable as this may sound, the citizens of Molalla, Oregon, where Killingsworth lives, have tried to ban this book from the school library for what they see as "logger bashing," so great apparently is their love affair with tree stumps, ugliness, and the chain saw.   **144 pp.; 1993**

23. *Angel Face*   **Norma Klein**

This subject is increasingly faced by young adult readers. Jason Lieberman's father leaves home for a woman called Randall Wormwood Hamilton; his mother goes ballistic; he falls in love with his classmate Vicki; and the family balance tips.   **208 pp.; 1984**

24. *A Wrinkle in Time*   **Madeleine L'Engle**

Won the Newberry Award thirty years ago and still going strong. This story of the adventures in space and time of Meg, Charles, and Calvin, as they search for Meg's father, a scientist who has disappeared, is itself timeless. In *A Ring of Endless Light* fifteen-year-old Vicky, whose grandfather is dying of leukemia, finds comfort with the pod of dolphins on whom she has been doing research.   **211 pp.; 1962**

25. *Tell Me a Story*   **Chase Collins Levey**

Subtitled *Creating Bedtime Tales Your Children Will Dream On*, this is a practical guide to developing a good story and making it your own, tailored to your child's questions, fears, and dreams. A great idea.   **179 pp.; 1992**

26. *Pippi Longstocking*   **Astrid Lindgren**

Hooray, a young adult book with no disease, divorce, death, child abuse, or pollution. Lindgren created this red-haired delight—who lives alone in Sweden without parents, but with a horse on the porch, a pet monkey, and a treasure of gold pieces—for her sick daughter. *Pippi Goes on Board* and *Pippi in the South Seas* followed.   **160 pp.; 1945**

27. *The Brave*   **Robert Lipsyte**

Seventeen-year-old Sonny Bear comes from the reservation of the Moscondaga Nation, but when he lands in New York City, Alfred Brooks, a cop and the hero of *The Contender*, is the one who protects him. In *The Chief*, the finale in this trilogy, it is Sonny Bear's Harlem sidekick, Martin Witherspoon, who saves the day.   **208 pp.; 1991**

28. *Anastasia Krupnik*   **Lois Lowry**

All of Lowry's award-winning books about this delightful ten-year-old are highly recommended. Lowry faces the issues of the day without drenching the reader in sorrow and helplessness since Anastasia is surrounded by a loving if slightly eccentric family. Lowry's books about Anastasia's brother, Sam, are equally wonderful. Some in the series are *Anastasia Again!*; *Anastasia at Your Service*; *Anastasia, Ask Your Analyst*; *Anastasia on Her Own*; *Anastasia Has the Answers*; *Anastasia's Chosen Career*, and *All About Sam*.

                                                        113 pp.; 1979

29. *Sarah, Plain and Tall*   **Patricia MacLachlan**

Many kids know this one from the TV production. The father of Caleb and Anna invites a mail-order bride to come live with them on the prairie. She turns out—in a twist on the usual story—to be the perfect stepmother.   **58 pp.; 1987**

30. *Anne of Green Gables*   **Lucy Maude Montgomery**

The skinny freckled redhead named Anne Shirley who arrives on Prince Edward Island first appeared eighty-five years ago.

By 1943 it had gone through forty-four printings and was followed by *Anne of Avonlea*, *Chronicles of Avonlea*, *Anne of
the Island*, *Anne of Windy Poplars*, *Anne's House of Dreams*,
and *Anne of Ingleside*. These books are favorites of readers
around the world, and, even today, Montgomery's farmhouse
is treated like a shrine, particularly by the Japanese.

309 pp.; 1908

31. *Now Is Your Time*   **William Dean Myers**
Subtitled *The African-American Struggle for Freedom*. This
book, selected by the American Library Association as a
Notable Children's Book in 1991 and as one of the Best
Books for Young Adults in 1992, focuses on nearly three cen-
turies of African-American experience. *Scorpions* is about a
Harlem gang, a boy named Jamal, and guns.   292 pp.; 1991

32. *Shiloh*   **Phyllis Reynolds Naylor**
Marty finds a lost beagle in the hills behind his West Virginia
home. He tries to hide it both from his family and the dog's
meanspirited owner, who shoots deer out of season and mis-
treats animals.   144 pp.; 1991

33. *Lyddie*   **Katherine Paterson**
The industrial revolution in America, specifically the mills of
Lowell, Massachusetts in the mid-1840s, provide the setting
for the endurance of Lydia Worthen. *Bridge to Terabithia* is
about a ten-year-old boy in rural Virginia whose friend meets
an untimely death. Also *Jacob Have I Loved* and *The Great
Gilly Hopkins*.   102 pp.; 1991

34. *Hatchet*   **Gary Paulson**
A plane crash causes thirteen-year-old Brian to spend fifty-
four days in the wilderness, learning to survive initially with
only the hatchet given to him by his mother. He survives his
parents' divorce as well. In *Dogsong*, a fourteen-year-old
Eskimo boy takes a 1,400-mile journey by dog sled, seeking
his own "song." Also *The Winter Room*.   195 pp.; 1987

35. *Tar Beach*   **Faith Ringgold**
Cassie Louise Lightfoot dreams of floating over a 1930s New

York City and wearing the George Washington Bridge for a necklace. Based on the author's quilt painting of the same name.   **32 pp.; 1991**

36. *The Weirdo*   Theodore Taylor
Voted the American Library Association's Best Young Adult Book. Samantha finally meets the Weirdo, and together they search for the killer who stalks innocent victims in the swamp. Taylor wrote *The Cay*, the story of a white boy blinded by a blow to the head and of an old black man from whom he acquires a new kind of vision.   **224 pp.; 1991**

37. *Dicey's Song*   Cynthia Voigt
Dicey Tillerman manages to reach her grandmother's run-down farm on Chesapeake Bay with her three younger siblings in tow. Like many children today, she has a lot of responsibility for one so young. In *Homecoming* the four of them, with eleven dollars to their names, walk to their aunt's house in Connecticut. *A Solitary Blue* is about the return of Jeff's mother, who deserted the family years ago, and the boy's relationship with his father.   **196 pp.; 1982**

38. *A Visit to William Blake's Inn*   Nancy Willard
A collection of poems with illustrations by Alice and Martin Provensen describing the curious group of guests who arrive at the supposed inn of the poet William Blake, who lived from 1757 to 1827. Also *Beauty and the Beast.*

44 pp.; 1981

39. *The Star Fisher*   Lawrence Yep
Yep won the Newberry for *Dragonwings*, a wonderful book about a Chinese-American boy and his father in San Francisco. Here Yep uses the experiences of his grandparents, mother, aunts, and uncles, who were the first Chinese family to settle in Clarksburg, Virginia. The star fisher bird, a magical creature who is half bird and half woman, is a symbol here for the stress immigrants feel when their children turn into Americans.   **150 pp.; 1991**

40. *The Pigman & Me*   **Paul Zindel**
This recalls Zindel's teenage years on Staten Island when his
life is enriched by finding his own personal pigman, or men-
tor. Also *The Pigman*.   **178 pp.; 1992**

SO WHAT'S NEW?

1. *Closing Arguments*   **Frederick Busch**
His fifteenth novel; a dark and complicated work about sex, violence, child abuse, and the law. *Long Way from Home* followed.   **304 pp.; 1991**

2. *The Wrestler's Cruel Study*   **Stephen Dobyns**
Are we hearing Nietzsche here? No, it's a postmodern novel featuring a wrestler's manager who thinks like him.
      426 pp.; 1993

3. *Consider This, Señora*   **Harriet Doerr**
Fans of *Stones for Ibarra* have been waiting a long time for this one. Set again in Mexico, this novel examines the lives of a group of American expatriates who face some big adjustments.   **241 pp.; 1993**

4. *Arc d'X*   **Steve Erickson**
A hallucinatory narrative that begins with a love affair between good old Thomas Jefferson and his slave Sally Hemings. There is (of course) a character named Erickson, who, like the author, was born in Los Angeles and moved to Paris. If you like Thomas Pynchon, you'll love Erickson.
      288 pp.; 1993

5. *Like Water for Chocolate*   **Laura Esquivel**
Love, hope, sex, and recipes, all on a Mexican ranch.
246 pp.; 1992

6. *The Virgin Suicides*   **Jeffrey Eugenides**
Eugenides wrote this first novel when his fifteen-year-old baby-sitter told him that she and her five sisters had each attempted suicide. The possibilities are nightmarish.
249 pp.; 1993

7. *Sarah Canary*   **Karen Joy Fowler**
Quirky, bizarre, and wonderful American quest novel, set in the Washington Territory in 1873. Definitely a writer to watch! **290 pp.; 1991**

8. *Virtual Light*   **William Gibson**
Gibson founded the cyberpunk movement; this is his new futuristic novel, a tale about the consequences of virtual reality. **325 pp.; 1993**

9. *Henry James's Midnight Song*   **Carol De Chellis Hill**
Murdered women and dismembered corpses. The suspects include Freud, Wilhelm Fliess, Emma Eckstein (Fliess's patient), Ida Bauer, the patient described by Freud as Dora, Carl Gustav Jung, Sabina Spielrein (Jung's patient and lover), Edith Wharton, Henry James, and a Countess von Gerzl, with whom Viennese Inspector Maurice Cheval LeBlanc has fallen in love. Hooray! **445 pp.; 1993**

10. *Force of Gravity*   **R. S. Jones**
Terrifying tale of a descent into insanity as Emmet Barfield grows smaller. A new talent for the strong of stomach.
320 pp.; 1991

11. *Max in Hollywood, Baby*   **Maira Kalman**
Max Stravinsky, canine extraordinaire, was in Paris recently—see *Ooh-la-la (Max in Love)*—but in this one he's hanging with the West Coast crowd. His limo is, thankfully, chauffeured by Ferrrnando Extra Debonnaire. **32 pp.; 1992**

12. *The Body in Four Parts*   Janet Kauffman

The narrator-protagonist is four people in one—composed of the four basic elements (earth, fire, air, and water) that are personified as characters. Very interesting and unusual.

128 pp.; 1993

13. *Et, Tu, Babe*   Mark Leyner

Some more of the wild literature of the 1990s by the author of *My Cousin, My Gastroenterologist*.   168 pp.; 1992

14. *All the Pretty Horses*   Cormac McCarthy

Winner of both the National Book Award and the National Book Critics Circle Award, the story of a sixteen-year-old east Texan who leaves home in 1950, heads for Mexico, ends up in prison, and returns to Texas wiser but forever scarred. Two early books are *Child of God* and *Outer Dark*.

302 pp.; 1992

15. *Foxfire: Confessions of a Girl Gang*   Joyce Carol Oates

In her twenty-second novel Oates goes back to the 1950s when the women in an upstate New York town seek revenge. Dark and wonderful.   328 pp.; 1993

16. *Face*   Cecile Pineda

Not newly published, this novel, nominated for the American Book Award for first work, is about disfigurement, desertion, and the individual notion of self. In using these ideas Pineda was ahead of her time. Based on a true-life story.

194 pp.; 1985

17. *Love Is Strange*   Joel Rose and
                                              Catherine Texier (editors)

Stories of postmodern romance by fifteen writers who explore the emotional landscapes—from deepest downtown New York to decadent California.   288 pp.; 1993

18. *Nobody's Fool*   Richard Russo

This third novel is about Sully, a northern redneck in the town of North Bath, New York. And the allegorical content is provocative too.   576 pp.; 1993

19. *Iona Moon*   Melanie Rae Thon
Lush, beautiful, lyrical language about a supersensual wounded angel.   320 pp.; 1993

20. *Motion Sickness*   Lynne Tillman
A nameless woman travels to Paris, London, Istanbul, Italy, and Greece. Why she is traveling we don't know but, after all, this is postmodernism.   204 pp.; 1991

21. *Thirteen Stories and*   William T. Vollmann
Thirteen Epitaphs
As the *New York Times* reviewer said, this new collection of stories "can be read as a feverish contemporary travelogue . . . of Mr. Vollmann's brain." More than anything else, loss of place is the issue here. Vollmann wrote *The Rainbow Stories* and *Whores for Gloria*.   318 pp.; 1991

22. *The Women of Whitechapel*   Paul West
and Jack the Ripper
In 1888 a madman was on the loose in London and preying on the prostitutes of the Whitechapel district. A shocking, dark thriller about Jack's victims.   420 pp.; 1991

23. *Close to the Knives*   David Wojnarowicz
Subtitled *A Memoir of Disintegration*. Wojnarowicz, now deceased, witnesses among other things the gradual decay of close friend Peter Hujar, who has AIDS, and the sham doctor who prescribes typhoid injections. Not for the fainthearted.   288 pp.; 1991

24. *Tony and Susan*   Austin Wright
Combines a stark take on a film noir theme with a postmodern meditation on the art of reading.   334 pp.; 1993

IN THE HAMMOCK

1. *Sisters and Lovers*   **Connie Briscoe**
Beverly, Charmaine, and Evelyn are three sisters living in Washington, D.C.—one with a perfect husband, one reluctantly single, and one with a useless husband. Briscoe, who is deaf, is the managing editor of *American Annals of the Deaf* at Gallaudet University.   **352 pp.; 1993**

2. *The Way to Cook*   **Julia Child**
While you're lying there—not exercising or mowing the grass—you may as well read about all the butter, sugar, and cholesterol you are no longer allowed to eat. Child has been my hero since the day she said, "Life itself is the proper binge."   **544 pp.; 1989**

3. *Snagged*   **Carol Higgins Clark**
Her second Regan Reilly mystery, this one takes place in South Miami Beach where two conventions—one for panty hose manufacturers, one for representatives of the funeral industry—are meeting at the same hotel. Very funny book with a great title!   **227 pp.; 1993**

4. *Jurassic Park*   **Michael Crichton**
Gives all of us past the dinosaur stage a chance to indulge our continuing fascination with them. The plot also serves our

more grown-up interest in genetics, DNA, and the rest. Your reading club can always get a discussion going with *Rising Sun*. 399 pp.; 1990

5. *Having Our Say* Sarah and A. Elizabeth Delany
Subtitled *The Delany Sisters' First 100 Years*. Written with the journalist Amy Hill Hearth, here Bessie (now 102) and Sarah (104) share wisdom on everything from the "old Rebby boys" of their North Carolina childhood to the 1865 "Surrender" ("the way Papa always referred to the end of the Civil War"). The sisters Delany, never-married daughters of this country's first black Episcopal bishop, grew up to be the first black home economics teacher in a New York City high school (Sadie), and, with a D.D.S. from Columbia, the second black female dentist licensed in New York City (Bessie).
210 pp.; 1993

6. *The Rabbi of Lud* Stanley Elkin
Winner of the 1983 National Book Critics Circle Award for *George Mills*, Elkin here writes a funny book about Rabbi Goldkorn, formerly Chief Rabbi of the Alaskan Pipeline (and we know how big *that* congregation must have been!), and now the rebbe in residence at a cemetery in Lud, New Jersey. Three wonderful novellas make up *Van Gogh's Room at Arles*. 277 pp.; 1986

7. *The Pelican Brief* John Grisham
A good read about a law student who looks into the murder of two Supreme Court justices. 436 pp.; 1992

8. *Never Sleep with a Fat Man in July* Modine Gunch
Now *this* is a funny book—all about life with Lout, his son Gargoyle, Miss Larva, and the other Gunches, by the author of *Never Heave Your Bosom in a Front-Hook Bra*.
117 pp.; 1993

9. *Final Argument* Clifford Irving
A compelling courtroom drama that focuses on a black man falsely accused of murder and the lawyer who becomes obsessed with the case. 356 pp.; 1993

10. *After All These Years*   **Susan Isaacs**
The now very rich Rosie Myers, dumped by husband Richie
the morning after their twenty-fifth wedding anniversary, is
busy stuffing her face in her mansion on Long Island. On the
way to the kitchen she trips over a dead body. One guess as to
whose it is.   **343 pp.; 1993**

11. *Molly Ivins Can't Say That, Can She?*   **Molly Ivins**
In my next life I plan to come back as this hilarious, right-on-
target political writer for the *Fort Worth Star-Telegram*. Her
new book is Nothin' *but* Good *Times Ahead*.   **294 pp.; 1991**

12. *Moosewood Cookbook*   **Mollie Katzen**
Vegetarian meals with less oil, and fewer eggs and dairy prod-
ucts, from the great Ithaca restaurant maven. Your cardiolo-
gist will prefer the revised version.   **227 pp.; 1977**

13. *Misery*   **Stephen King**
Sometimes those fans just turn ugly, and the writer Paul Shel-
don is in big trouble when he runs into one of them: Annie
Wilkes. For my money, this is King's best book.
                                                     310 pp.; 1987

14. *Salaryman*   **Meg Pei**
Jun Shimada is a "salaryman," a Japanese corporate climber
with a self-effacing dedication to his company. When he gets
to America, however, he falls off the ladder.   **296 pp.; 1992**

15. *Belinda*   **Anne Rampling (Anne Rice)**
Great read about dolls, attics, and a not quite kosher love
affair. One of my favorites.   **439 pp.; 1988**

16. *Outer Banks*   **Anne Rivers Siddons**
Kate Abrams, a successful interior designer approaching fifty,
agrees to an informal reunion with her three college roommates at a summer home on the Outer Banks of North Carolina. Siddons wrote *Peachtree Road*.   **401 pp.; 1991**

17. *Dreams Like Thunder*   **Diane Simmons**
Ten-year-old Alberta tells this 1959 story of life on a small

eastern Oregon farm between Baker and Hells Canyon. An endearing, touching story.   189 pp.; 1992

18. *The Shadow of the Shadow*   Paco Ignacio Taibo II
A spellbinding novel that takes place in 1922 in Mexico City, where a group of intellectuals gets caught up in a political conspiracy.   288 pp.; 1991

19. *Anatomy of a Murder*   Robert Traver
Both the murder and the trial take place on the "water-hemmed" Upper Peninsula of Michigan, a wild, harsh and broken land.   437 pp.; 1958

20. *Presumed Innocent*   Scott Turow
Rusty Sabich, a chief deputy prosecutor, investigates the rape and murder of Carolyn Polhemus, his colleague and former lover. Suddenly, he becomes the accused.   431 pp.; 1987

21. *Finnegan's Week*   Joseph Wambaugh
Finbar Finnegan, a San Diego detective, who is "a failed actor, a failed cop and the world's worst marriage prospect," says his third ex-wife "needed a metal tag on her ear just so I could follow her migration habits." Wambaugh's taste for the excessive, however, works here.   348 pp.; 1993

DREAM LISTS

Reading is one passion that all writers share. Because they know how difficult the writing process is, they are also passionate about what and whom they read. Here are a few dream lists (containing books not annotated elsewhere in this collection), generously supplied by some very fine writers:

* * *

Margot Livesey, born in Scotland but a resident of Massachusetts, is the author of *Learning By Heart*, a collection of short stories (see "Family Feuds"), and the novel *Homework*. She recommends:

Lady Audley's Secret   **Mary Elizabeth Braddon**
An old-fashioned Victorian page-turner in which the plot hooks us in the opening pages and never lets up.

Winter's Tales   **Isak Dinesen**
These beautiful, lucid stories remind us of the pleasures of the imagination—of knowing that something is just a story and enjoying it for just that reason. The gross question of plausibility never raises its toadlike head.

The Wars   **Timothy Findley**
This novel about a young Canadian soldier's experiences in France is remarkable for making new the horror of war. The protagonist, Robert Ross, makes an irresistible and completely surprising protest against the war.

Sunset Song   **Lewis Grassick Gibbon**
A highly evocative novel that follows the life of a spirited girl

growing up on a small Scottish farm before and during World War I. The exquisite descriptions of the dour landscape and of what it means to work the land are matched by the psychological subtlety.

* * *

Sylvia Watanabe, a Hawaiian who now lives in Michigan, is the author of a short story collection called *Talking to the Dead* (see "From Asian Shores"). She suggests:

Through the Safety Net	Charles Baxter
St. Augustine's Pigeon	Evan Connell
Childhood and Other Neighborhoods	Stuart Dybek
The Golden Notebook	Doris Lessing
The Pine Barrens	John McPhee
No Mercy	Lee Upton
The Lotus Flowers	Ellen Bryant Voigt

* * *

Angela Davis-Gardner, a native of North Carolina, is the author of the novels *Forms of Shelter* (see "Southern Comfort") and *Felice*. She likes:

Postcards   E. Annie Proulx
This novel is about a murderer's exile and the family and landscape he leaves behind in Vermont. Proulx recently won the National Book Award for *The Shipping News*.

Professor Romeo   Anne Bernays
A mordantly witty portrayal of a man incapable of fidelity. Yet somehow Bernays manages to make him a sympathetic character.

Sounding the Territory   Laurel Goldman
A very funny, wise, and brilliantly written novel about a confused young man who is figuring out how to live. Her second novel, *A Part of Fortune*, is set in a nursing home.

Revelation   **Peggy Payne**
A liberal minister, much in distress, hears the voice of God.

The Magic We Do Here   **Larry Rudner**
The warm, almost magical voice of the narrator, determined
to preserve the memories of the people he has known, tells
the story of the extermination of the Polish Jews.

The Second War   **G. C. Hendricks**
One of the best books available on Vietnam.

Home and Away   **Peter Filene**
A wonderful novel about a Jewish boy growing up in New
York; baseball is just one of its concerns.

Heading West   **Doris Betts**
A meek librarian is kidnapped in the Appalachian mountains
and finds herself on a perilous and enlightening journey. Betts
is also the author of a short story collection called *Beasts of
the Southern Wild*.

Music of the Swamp   **Lewis Nordan**
Wild and magical stories of Sugar Mecklin in the Delta. *Wolf
Whistle*, about the murder of Emmett Till, is recent.

I Am One of You Forever   **Fred Chappell**
In the South we consider Chappell to be one of our very best
writers. He wrote *More Shapes Than One*, a short story collection, and won the Bollingen Prize for poetry.

* * *

Jill McCorkle, a North Carolinian, (now living in Boston)
whose most recent book is *Crash Diet* (see "Southern Comfort"), offers these choices:

Other Voices, Other Rooms   **Truman Capote**
Don't forget the story called "A Christmas Memory."

Where She Brushed Her Hair   Max Steele
A short story collection that includes "The Cat and the Coffee Drinkers."

The Heart Is a Lonely Hunter   Carson McCullers

A Curtain of Green and Other Stories   Eudora Welty
The story, "A Memory," in particular.

The Story of My Life   Helen Keller

Diary of a Young Girl   Anne Frank

AUTHOR INDEX

TITLE INDEX

Dear Reader,
Did we miss any of your favorite books? Please let us know.

1.
2.
3.
4.
5.

(name)
(address)

Send to: Mickey Pearlman, Ph.D.
author of *What to Read*
c/o HarperCollins Publishers
10 East 53rd Street
New York, NY 10022